RODALE'S
SUCCESSFUL ORGANIC GARDENING™
LOW-MAINTENANCE
LANDSCAPING

RODALE'S
SUCCESSFUL ORGANIC GARDENING™
LOW-MAINTENANCE LANDSCAPING

TEXT BY ERIN HYNES

"LANDSCAPE SOLUTIONS" AND PLANT BY PLANT GUIDES BY SUSAN McCLURE

Rodale Press, Emmaus, Pennsylvania

Copyright © 1994 by Weldon Russell Pty Ltd

If you have any questions or comments concerning this book, please write to:

Rodale Press
Book Readers' Service
33 East Minor Street
Emmaus, PA 18098

Library of Congress Cataloging-in-Publication Data

Hynes, Erin.
  Low-maintenance landscaping / text by Erin Hynes ; landscape solutions and plant by plant guides by Susan McClure.
    p.   cm. — (Rodale's successful organic gardening)
  Includes index.
  ISBN 0–87596–613–6 hardcover — ISBN 0–87596–614–4 paperback
  1. Landscape gardening. 2. Low maintenanace gardening.
  3. Landscape plants. 4. Organic gardening. I. McClure, Susan.
  I. Title. II. Series.
  SB473.H96 1994
  712'.6—dc20   93–21425
                                        CIP

Produced by Mandarin Offset, Hong Kong

Printed in Hong Kong on acid-free paper

Rodale Press Staff:
    Executive Editor: Margaret Lydic Balitas
    Managing Editor: Barbara W. Ellis
    Editor: Nancy J. Ondra
    Copy Editor: Carolyn R. Mandarano

Produced for Rodale Press by Weldon Russell Pty Ltd
107 Union Street, North Sydney NSW 2060, Australia
a member of the Weldon International Group of Companies

    Publisher: Elaine Russell
    Publishing Manager: Susan Hurley
    Managing Editor: Ariana Klepac
    Senior Editor: Margaret Whiskin
    Editorial Assistant: Libby Frederico
    Copy Editor: Yani Silvana
    Designer: Rowena Sheppard
    Picture Researcher: Anne Nicol
    Photographers: John Callanan, David Wallace
    Illustrators: Barbara Rodanska, Jan Smith
    Macintosh Layout Artist: Edwina Ryan
    Indexer: Michael Wyatt
    Production Manager: Dianne Leddy

A KEVIN WELDON PRODUCTION

Distributed in the book trade by St. Martin's Press

2 4 6 8 10 9 7 5 3 1 hardcover
2 4 6 8 10 9 7 5 3 1 paperback

Opposite: Iceplant (*Mesembryanthemum* sp.)
Half title: Crocus
Opposite title page: Garden with alpines and conifers
Title page: *Chrysanthemum* 'Purple Rockery'
Opposite contents: Persian parrotia (*Parrotia persica*)
Back cover: *Helictotrichon sempervirens* and *Rudbeckia fulgida*
    var. *sullivantii* (middle), *Hosta crispula* (bottom)

CONTENTS

INTRODUCTION

You've always wanted a great-looking landscape—flower gardens filled with colorful blooms to brighten the yard or bring indoors; trees and shrubs for shade and privacy; vegetables and fruits to eat, store, or share; and a patch of lush green lawn for the kids and pets to play on. But who can have all that without spending every free minute raking, mowing, weeding, and watering? You can!

With some planning and a little know-how, it's easy to cut down on the drudgery of yard work. Maybe you'll use the time you save mowing the yard to concentrate on growing extra-special flowers or prize-winning vegetables. Or perhaps you'd just like to lie around the pool and admire your beautiful yard. We're sure you'll figure out something to do with all the time you save. While your neighbors are out every weekend trimming their hedges for the umpteenth time or plodding along behind the lawn mower, you can wave cheerfully as you head off to have fun.

If you've been looking for ways to cut down on yard work, you may have resigned yourself to covering your garden with plastic mulch and crushed rocks or to replacing your lawn with sweeps of ivy, pachysandra, and periwinkle. If that's what you want to do, that's fine. But having an easy-care landscape doesn't have to be a matter of settling for second best. It's about deciding what you really want from your yard and what you're willing to do for it, then developing a realistic plan for making the two meet.

Whether you're starting from a featureless lot or adapting an established yard, this book is your guide to reducing or eliminating the maintenance chores you hate the most. From low-maintenance lawns to easy-care flower and vegetable gardens, you'll be able to apply timesaving techniques to every part of your landscape. Plus, you'll learn how to care for your plants and keep them healthy with safe, effective, environmentally friendly materials. So read on, and find out how you can create your own lush, livable landscape that looks great with a minimum of maintenance.

Opposite: If lawn mowing is a chore you dread, consider replacing at least part of the grass with wildflowers. Once you get them established, a few hours of weeding per year and an annual mowing will keep them looking good.

HOW TO USE THIS BOOK

odale's Successful Organic Gardening: Low-maintenance Landscaping is your guide to creating the landscape you've always wanted without committing yourself to years of weekend servitude to mowers, trimmers, and tillers. In these pages, you'll find tips and techniques for reducing maintenance in all parts of your yard, from lawns and flower beds to trees and food gardens.

Simple Steps to a Low-care Landscape

For easy reference, this book is divided into two basic sections. The first two chapters show you how to make the transition from your existing yard to the low-maintenance landscape of your dreams. "Taking a Look at Your Landscape," starting on page 12, helps you recognize the advantages and challenges of your site. You'll learn how features like soil, climate, topography, and exposure influence how much maintenance you have to do. You'll discover how to take advantage of the good conditions your site offers and how to cope with the challenges using techniques like terracing and proper plant selection.

"Moving Toward Low Maintenance," starting on page 22, shows the way to create a landscape plan that fits your budget and the time you can devote to installing and maintaining it. You'll find specific tips for turning an undeveloped lot into a great-looking, easy-care yard. If you already have a high-maintenance landscape, there's a whole section on adapting an existing yard to low-care techniques. A special feature of this chapter is the "Landscape Solutions Guide," starting on page 28. If you have special landscape challenges—like steep slopes, wet spots, or rocky areas—turn to this section to find photos and suggestions for effective, low-maintenance options.

Super Solutions for Specific Sites

The second part of this book is your guide to reducing maintenance in particular parts of the yard. Lawns, for instance, can be a pleasure or a pain, depending on how you maintain them. "Easy-care Lawns and Groundcovers," starting on page 40, tells you how to create a lawn you can live with or, if you wish, how to replace some of it with something less demanding. It includes ways to minimize the time you spend mowing, edging, watering, and fertilizing your grass. "Low-maintenance Groundcovers," starting on page 48, is a plant-by-plant guide to growing over 15 great groundcover plants.

We may curse our lawns, but we love our trees and shrubs for the shade, shape, texture, and color they add to our surroundings. In "Timesaving Trees and Shrubs," starting on page 58, you'll learn how to choose, plant, and take care of these easy ornamentals. The plant-by-plant guide for this chapter, "Low-maintenance Trees and Shrubs," starting on page 68, offers growing guidelines, problem-prevention tips, and planting suggestions for over 40 easy-care landscape plants.

While trees and shrubs give substance and serenity to the landscape, flowers add excitement and surprise. "Quick and Colorful Flower Gardens," starting on page 90, covers flowers gardens for both sunny and shady yards. It gives tips on designing flower beds that blend colors, shapes, and sizes in ways that please the eye. "Low-maintenance Flowers," starting on page 100, includes information on growing over 45 easy annuals and perennials.

With all the time you're saving not caring for the yard, you'll have more time to enjoy the fruits (and vegetables) of your labor. "Effortless Edibles," starting on page 124, tells you how to grow all sorts of good things to eat, including vegetables, herbs, and small fruit like blueberries and strawberries. It includes pointers on getting the most harvest for the least effort and a handy care calendar covering each season in the vegetable garden. "Low-maintenance Edibles," starting on page 138, is the place to go for growing tips on over 30 favorite easy-care food crops.

Using the Plant-by-Plant Guides

The encyclopedic guides at the end of these chapters are arranged alphabetically by the plant names. Entries for edible crops—herbs, vegetables, and fruits—are alphabetical by common name. Ornamental plants—groundcovers, trees and shrubs, and flowers—are alphabetical by their botanical names. (Buying an ornamental plant by its botanical name is really the only way to make sure you get the right one. Many common names apply to more than one plant, and all of those plants may not be ideal for low-maintenance landscapes.) If you want to find information on a specific ornamental plant but only know it by a common name, look it up in the Index and you'll be directed to the right place to look.

For each plant, you'll find information about the best climate and site to help you determine if the plant will thrive in your conditions. Growing guidelines cover basic care information, along with any special cultural tips. You'll learn what problems the plant might be prone to and how to prevent them. Color photographs accompany each entry to help you choose plants you find attractive or identify those you already have.

By providing all the information you need to select the most care-free plants and grow them successfully, the plant-by-plant guides will help you create the most low-maintenance landscape possible. The diagram below shows what to look for on these informative pages.

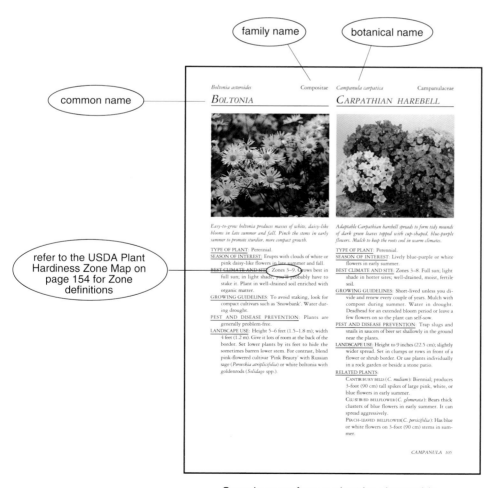

Sample page from a plant by plant guide.

TAKING A LOOK AT
YOUR LANDSCAPE

Creating a low-maintenance garden doesn't mean settling for acres of plain green groundcovers or boring expanses of gravel. You can have a great-looking garden, one that fits right in with the neighborhood—except you won't have to spend nearly as much time as your neighbors do to keep your yard looking great.

Knowing the physical characteristics of your site—the soil, climate, topography, and exposure—is a vital part of creating and maintaining a low-maintenance landscape. If you're starting from scratch, you'll use this information to choose well-adapted plants and to design a functional, attractive layout for your yard. If you already have a landscape, investigating its physical characteristics can give you valuable insight into ways to eliminate work you're doing now or to gradually adjust the amount of maintenance your site requires.

A big part of making your garden low maintenance comes from working with the plants and conditions you have rather than from struggling to make poorly adapted plants grow. Plants are healthiest—and require the least care from you—when they're well suited to the region and site where you plant them. In the cool, humid Northeast, it's a snap to grow woodland wildflowers in shady spots. In the southwestern United States, lavender cottons (*Santolina* spp.), penstemons (*Penstemon* spp.), and other heat- and drought-tolerant plants will thrive with little extra care.

Putting plants where they don't belong can lead to real headaches. Firs (*Abies* spp.), for instance, may grow well in cool Northern areas, but they tend to be weak and plagued with problems in hot-summer climates. With plenty of extra care, you can sometimes force a plant to grow where it's not well adapted, but that's not low maintenance. Knowing what growing conditions your site has to offer will help you avoid potential problem plants and pick ones that will grow and look great with a minimum of coddling.

In this chapter, you'll learn how to identify your garden conditions—from the soil texture to the topography—and how they relate to creating a low-maintenance landscape. Some factors, like climate, affect your whole yard; others, like the amount of sun or shade, can differ widely as you walk around the house. It's helpful to know how conditions vary in different areas, so you can put plants in just the right spots. As you learn about your site, jot down your findings in a notebook. These details will be very handy when you're planning new plantings or thinking about a new lower-care layout for your yard.

Opposite: A low-maintenance landscape doesn't have to be dull. Choosing easy-care plants and putting them in the right conditions will go a long way toward reducing maintenance chores, like pruning and controlling pests.

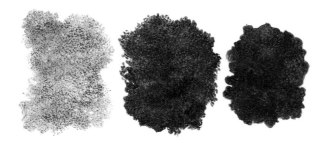

Study the Soil

Gardening can be a breeze if you have deep, fertile soil rich in organic matter. But even if you don't (and very few of us do), you can still have a beautiful, productive, low-maintenance yard. You may decide to improve the soil you have—by adding organic matter or building raised beds, for instance—or you may just look for plants that are adapted to the existing conditions. Either way, you'll need to know a few basic things about the soil you're starting with.

Texture

When gardeners start rattling on about clays, sands, silts, and loams, they're talking about soil texture. Texture refers to the relative percentages of the

Not all plants need moist, fertile soil. In fact, calendulas will grow just fine in dry, average soil.

different-sized particles that make up a soil. Sand grains are the biggest particles, ranging in size from 0.05 to 2 millimeters. Silt particles are ten times smaller than the finest sand; clay particles are ten times smaller than silt.

Most soils are a mix of the three different particle groups. The ideal soil is a loam, with a ratio of 40 percent sand, 40 percent silt, and 20 percent clay. Loam drains quickly, but not too quickly for plant roots to absorb water and nutrients. And the pores between the soil particles hold enough air for roots to get the oxygen they need.

As the percentages shift in

Low raised beds can provide ideal growing conditions for a variety of annual vegetables and flowers, including nasturtiums and lettuce.

A Hands-on Test for Soil Texture

This quick test will give you a good idea if your soil is sandy, silty, or clayey. Start by taking a chunk of soil about the size of your thumb. Moisten it enough that you can roll it into a ball. Flatten the ball between the pad of your thumb and the side of your bent index finger. Push your thumb forward repeatedly, pressing the soil outward to form a ribbon. The longer the ribbon, the more clay is in the soil. A heavy clay will make a ribbon 1 inch (2.5 cm) long; a sandy soil might not make a ribbon at all.

To confirm your findings, put the ribbon in your palm and add enough water to make a runny paste. Rub the index finger of your other hand around in the slop in your palm. If it feels gritty, the soil is sandy. If it's smooth, the soil is silty. If it's on the sticky side, you've got clay.

Clayey soils tend to hold lots of water, providing ideal conditions for moisture-loving plants like astilbes.

any direction, gardening becomes more challenging. Loose, sandy soils don't hold water and nutrients well; they'll need more frequent watering and fertilizing, unless you pick plants that are adapted to drier, infertile soil. Tight, clayey soils hold water too well, becoming soggy and hard to work. They can be ideal if you only grow moisture-loving plants like astilbes; otherwise, you'll probably want to loosen the soil with organic matter or build raised beds to improve drainage. Silty soils have some characteristics of both extremes, but tend to be more like clay than like sand. How and if you want to amend silty soil will depend on what plants you'd like to grow.

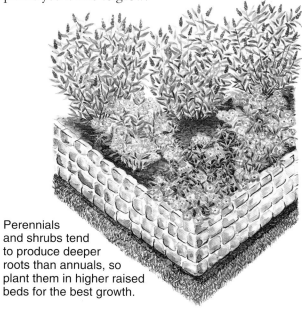

Perennials and shrubs tend to produce deeper roots than annuals, so plant them in higher raised beds for the best growth.

Soil Depth

The actual depth of your soil has an impact on root growth and in turn affects what plants can thrive on the site. In some regions, the soil is a thin dust over bedrock. In others, thousands of years worth of decayed prairie grasses have formed soils 6 feet (1.8 m) deep.

It's easy to tell which conditions you have—just dig in with a shovel. If you can go 2 feet (60 cm) without hitting a sheet of rock or a band of dense, tightly compacted soil, you'll be able to grow a wide range of

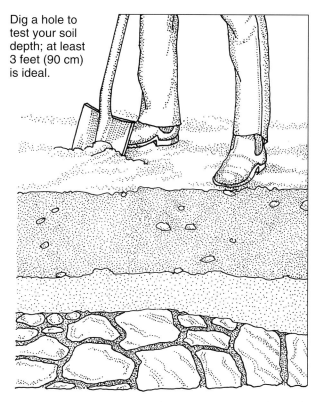

Dig a hole to test your soil depth; at least 3 feet (90 cm) is ideal.

Adding organic matter can improve almost any kind of soil, providing the best growing conditions for a healthy garden.

perennials, vegetables, herbs, and other shallow-rooted plants with little trouble. Larger plants, like shrubs and trees, generally need soil that's at least 3 feet (90 cm) deep (above rock or a dense, compacted layer) for healthy, vigorous growth.

Soils shallower than 2 feet (60 cm) above some limiting layer are less hospitable to good root growth; they may be prone to waterlogging, and they often have less nutrients than deeper soils. If your soil is shallow, you may decide to build raised beds and fill them with a good soil to provide more area for root growth. A 6-inch (15 cm) high bed should accommodate most vegetables and annual flowers; you'll need an 18- to 24-inch (45 to 60 cm) bed for perennials and smaller shrubs. (Raised beds can dry out quickly, though, so you may have to water them more frequently.) Or you could stick with more shallow-rooted plantings that are adapted to limited root zones.

Fertility

Fertility is the availability—not just the presence—of nutrients in the soil. Plants draw large amounts of nitrogen, phosphorus, potassium, sulfur, calcium, and magnesium from the soil. They also require traces of iron, boron, manganese, molybdenum, zinc, chlorine, copper, and nickel. Many of these nutrients are naturally released for plant use as mineral-rich rocks break down into soil.

Most plants grow best when the soil contains an ample supply of balanced nutrients, but some actually grow better if soil nutrients are low. Nitrogen-rich soils, for instance, will cause plants like yarrow and

Coreopsis grows best in soil that isn't very fertile; too much nitrogen can lead to weak stems that need staking.

> ## Taking a Soil Test
>
> If your existing plants have been growing well for years, you may not want to bother with a soil test. If you're starting a new landscape, or if your plants aren't thriving, it's worth taking a few minutes to collect some soil samples and get them tested. Do-it-yourself kits are available, but to get the most accurate picture of your soil's chemistry, you need a professional soil test.
>
> Your local Cooperative Extension Service office has instructions on soil testing. You can also contact a private soil-testing lab. The test results will tell you about your soil's fertility, pH, and organic-matter content. They may include suggestions on fertilizer types and amounts to apply to raise nutrient levels; don't forget to ask for organic recommendations. Take the time to really read the test results and to make the changes your soil needs. Getting your soil in shape before planting will go a long way toward promoting healthy, trouble-free plants in the future.

coreopsis to form lush, floppy growth that requires yearly staking. Grown in less fertile soil, the same plants may need almost no maintenance. Knowing the nutrient content of your soil will help you select the most appropriate plants for the conditions.

A soil test can tell you if your land has the right nutrients in the right balance for normal plant growth; see "Taking a Soil Test" for more information. If the results show that the pH is extreme or your soil is low in available nutrients, use an organic fertilizer to correct the problem. Use restraint when correcting a deficiency, though; too much fertilizer can easily be as bad as not enough. Follow the application rates given on the product label.

Organic Matter

Organic matter—basically decaying plant material, such as leaves and grass—is another important source of nutrients. Healthy soils usually have organic matter contents of 5 percent or more. Soils that are high in organic matter tend to be dark brown or black and have a loose, crumbly feel.

No matter what kind of soil you have, adding organic matter—in the form of compost, aged manure, chopped leaves, or other nutrient-rich materials—is

Inspect your garden soil each year—it should be loose and crumbly, with a healthy population of earthworms.

the number-one way to make it suitable for a wide range of plants. Organic matter improves garden soil by loosening up heavy clays (promoting better drainage) and increasing the water- and nutrient-holding capacities of sands (so you'll water and fertilize less frequently). Organic matter also encourages healthy populations of earthworms and other soil organisms, which in turn contribute nutrients and encourage root growth. All of these factors will lead to vigorous,

healthier plants that look great and are naturally more resistant to pest and disease problems.

pH

pH is the measure of how acid or alkaline your soil is. Acid soils have a pH below 7.0; alkaline soils, above 7.0. Soil with a pH of 7.0 is neutral.

The soil's pH has a great effect on its fertility. At certain pH ranges, some nutrients form chemical compounds that plants can't absorb through their roots. Iron, for example, is bound up in alkaline soils, while acid soils make potassium, calcium, and magnesium less available. Most nutrients tend to be fairly available at a pH of around 7.0.

Since it can be difficult to make significant long-term changes to soil pH, it's wise to look for plants that are adapted to your existing conditions; in the long run, these plants will be the most trouble-free. A pH of 6.5 to 7.0 will provide the right conditions for most plants, but there are some exceptions. Acid-lovers, like rhododendrons, mountain laurels (*Kalmia* spp.), and blueberries, grow best at a low pH (4.5 to 5.0); other plants, like baby's-breath (*Gypsophila* spp.) and cabbage, are better adapted to alkaline conditions. As you read plant descriptions in books and catalogs, keep an eye out for these exceptions, and avoid them if they don't match the conditions you have.

Composted garden trimmings and grass clippings will produce an excellent source of organic matter.

Baby's-breath grows best in alkaline soil, though it can tolerate garden soil with a pH near neutral.

Consider the Climate

Climate—the seasonal cycles of rainfall, temperatures, humidity, and other factors—has a major influence on which plants will thrive in your landscape. Some tough plants, like daylilies (*Hemerocallis* spp.) and hostas (*Hosta* spp.), can grow in a wide range of temperature and moisture conditions. Other plants can take varying temperatures but absolutely must have a certain amount of rainfall (or irrigation if the rains don't come).

All plants have a certain range of temperatures and moisture levels that they will grow best in. If you know what your garden has to offer, you can look for plants that are naturally adapted to those conditions and be fairly confident that they will grow well with a minimum of fuss on your part.

Think about Temperature

If you want to grow plants that will live for more than 1 year—including trees, shrubs, grasses, and perennials—you have to consider your area's average low and high temperatures. Plants that are naturally adapted to this temperature range will tend to survive and thrive in your landscape.

Most plant recommendations are based on an area's low temperatures. The United States Department of Agriculture has mapped each region's average winter low temperature on the USDA Plant Hardiness Zone Map. This map, reproduced on page 155, divides the continental United States and Canada into ten zones. Each zone has a minimum temperature that you can expect during the winter.

When you know what zone you live in, limit your selections to plants that are reliably cold-hardy for your area. Marginally hardy plants may survive for several years, but it's likely that they won't thrive, and an unusually cold spell can kill them off.

Summer high temperatures also limit which woody plants, flowers, and turf grasses you can grow. Even if a plant can tolerate the heat, it may demand frequent watering

Daylilies are hardy, durable plants that will produce showy, colorful blooms in many different climates.

in return, and it probably won't look great. Many delphiniums, for instance, will limp along in hot Southern summers and die out after 1 or 2 years, while the same plants in the North can grow and bloom for several years.

Plants that can't take the heat are a bad choice if you want a good-looking, easy-care garden. Unfortunately, it's difficult to put a number on a plant's heat tolerance. Plant descriptions in books and catalogs often suggest both lower and upper hardiness zone ranges (as in "Zones 5 to 8"). Use these recommendations as guidelines, but also check around local neighborhoods and botanical gardens to see how the plant actually performs in your area before you decide to include it in your landscape.

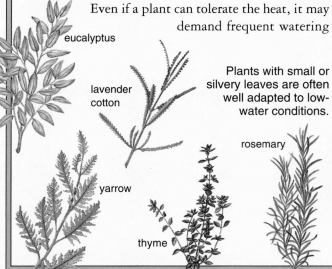

eucalyptus

lavender
cotton

Plants with small or silvery leaves are often well adapted to low-water conditions.

rosemary

yarrow

thyme

Sunny walls can provide a warm, protected microclimate that is ideal for heat-loving plants.

Moisture-loving plants like primroses and astilbes thrive in cool, humid climates with high rainfall.

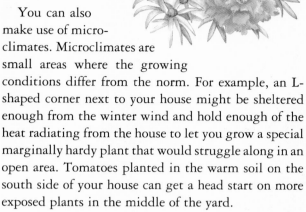

Rose moss (*Portulaca grandiflora*) is well suited for hot, dry sites.

Rainfall

Rainfall, like temperature, has a great impact on determining which plants will grow in an area without supplemental water. If you don't mind lugging hoses around for frequent watering or if you plan to have an automatic irrigation system, you may choose to grow plants that need extra water. If you want to grow just a few moisture-loving plants, site them close to the house where you can more easily give them special attention. But if your goal is to save time, money, and natural resources, you'll definitely want to include naturally adapted plants in your landscape.

Small, fuzzy, or silvery leaves—such as those on many herbs—are fairly reliable clues that a particular plant is adapted to low-water conditions. To get ideas on other plants that grow well in your region without extra water, see what's growing in local natural areas that have similar conditions to your yard. Your local Cooperative Extension Service may have suggestions of landscape plants for your area that don't need supplemental water. *Xeriscape Gardening* by Connie Ellefson, Tom Stephens, and Doug Welsh (Macmillan Publishing Company, 1992) also contains lists of adapted plants for various regions throughout the United States.

Coping with Your Climate

In most cases, your influence over the climate is limited, especially if you want a low-maintenance landscape. In dry regions or droughts, you can water your plants or install irrigation systems to do it for you. In rainy areas, you can plant in raised beds filled with sandy loam for better drainage.

You can also make use of microclimates. Microclimates are small areas where the growing conditions differ from the norm. For example, an L-shaped corner next to your house might be sheltered enough from the winter wind and hold enough of the heat radiating from the house to let you grow a special marginally hardy plant that would struggle along in an open area. Tomatoes planted in the warm soil on the south side of your house can get a head start on more exposed plants in the middle of the yard.

You can also work around your climate. If you grow vegetables in the Deep South, either plant early or late in the season or choose quick-maturing cultivars that produce their crop before the hottest summer months. Quick-growing cultivars are also ideal for cool, short-season areas. If you live where summers are humid and fungal diseases are common, look for ornamental species and cultivars that are naturally disease-resistant.

Remember that accepting and working with your climate is a key part of creating a low-maintenance yard. Experimenting with a few "touchy" plants can be fun, but make sure your landscape is mostly based on hardy plants that have proven themselves in your area. That way, you'll have a background of dependable, good-looking, easy-care plants to enjoy year-round.

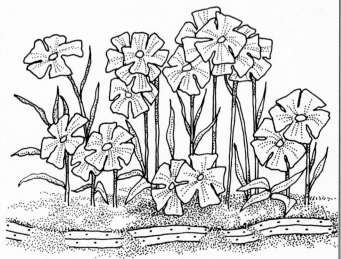

In dry climates, plants may need extra water. Combine soaker hoses and mulches for a low-maintenance solution.

Shrubs like creeping juniper (*Juniperus horizontalis*) and cinquefoil (*Potentilla* spp.) hold the soil on gentle slopes.

Reduce maintenance on tough-to-mow slopes by replacing turf with a mixture of lower-care wildflowers.

Think about the Topography

Topography is the lay of the land—its slopes, dips, and flat expanses. If you consider the topography of your site as you lay out the landscape, you'll save yourself a lot of future work by siting flower beds, lawn areas, vegetable gardens, and utility areas in the most appropriate, easy-to-reach spots.

Flatlands for Easy Care

For low-maintenance landscaping, level sites are ideal. On a completely level property, you won't even have to consider topography as you lay out your landscape. If only part of your property is flat, reserve it for recreation—perhaps a dining area or a play area for kids. Or use that area for flower gardens and an easy-to-mow lawn, and save the slopes for shrubs, trees, and groundcovers.

Coping with Slopes

Hills might be more pleasing to the eye than flat land,

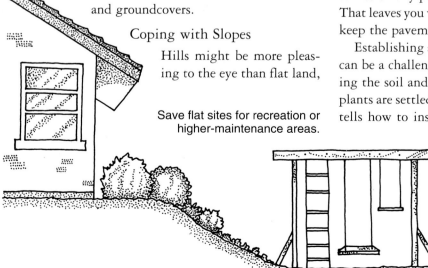

Save flat sites for recreation or higher-maintenance areas.

but they can make landscaping tougher. For one thing, it's a good deal harder to push a lawn mower up a hill than across a flat lawn. And the prospect of lugging a full garden cart uphill to a poorly placed compost pile is enough to overwhelm even the most dedicated gardener. As you lay out the different parts of your yard, always consider what sort of equipment access you'll need to maintain them. Try to site the more high-maintenance areas, like the vegetable garden, on level ground or the most gentle slopes.

How and what you plant on slopes also has a big effect on the maintenance you'll have to do. Slopes with sparse plantings are a prime target for erosion problems and accompanying soil deposits. Every time it rains, the exposed soil flows downhill with the water and settles on any pavement that might be at the bottom. That leaves you with frequent shoveling or sweeping to keep the pavement clean.

Establishing a good cover of plants on a sloping site can be a challenge, but it's worth the effort of preparing the soil and providing some extra water until the plants are settled in. ("Great Goundcovers" on page 47 tells how to install and maintain these hardworking landscape plants.) If your yard is steeply sloped, your best option may be to build a retaining wall or terraces to create flat, simple-to-maintain planting areas. While neither structure is easy to create, both can be easy to care for, and they greatly increase your choice of suitable plants.

Examine the Exposure

Exposure is the combination of the intensity (amount) and duration of the light your plants receive. While most plants are somewhat tolerant of varying light levels, they all need a certain amount of light to grow well. Some, like English ivy (*Hedera helix*) and Japanese pachysandra (*Pachysandra terminalis*), can take dense shade, with no direct sun; others, like lavender and eucalyptus, will sulk without a full day of sunshine. Siting your plants so they get the right amount of light is a key part of creating a low-maintenance landscape.

How Exposure Affects Plants

Plants are grouped by the intensity and duration of light they require. Full-sun plants, including most trees, flowers, and vegetables, can take the sun's full intensity all day. Partial-shade plants, such as columbines (*Aquilegia* spp.) and astilbes, need only 5 or 6 hours of direct light or a full day of light filtered by a tall tree. Shade plants, like most ferns, do well under trees, where no direct sun penetrates, or on the shady side of a building.

Columbines provide colorful late-spring flowers for shady gardens.

Many plants can take a range of full sun to part shade, or full shade to part shade, often depending on

Shady gardens don't have to be boring. Many showy easy-care plants—including astilbes and hostas—thrive there.

the light intensity. Light is more intense at high altitudes, where the atmosphere is thinner; in dry regions, where it's less humid; and in rural areas, where there's less air pollution. Light intensity also decreases as you travel farther from the equator. In areas with high light intensity, plants that normally need full sun—like many bellflowers (*Campanula* spp.)—often grow better in partial shade. Conversely, shade-loving plants like hostas may be able to take direct sun in low-intensity regions.

Consider Sun and Shade

In most cases, the best way to deal with the exposure of your yard is to just enjoy the sun or shade you have. If you have lots of shade, select from the wide variety of shade-loving foliage and flowering plants and be grateful for cool shade on hot summer days. If your yard receives unrelenting sun, plant some trees for the future, and build arbors or screens for more immediate shade. Or just bask in the sun and take advantage of the situation to grow vegetables, fruit, and sun-loving ornamentals. By placing your plants in the sites they prefer, you're giving them the right conditions to grow well with a minimum of extra care from you.

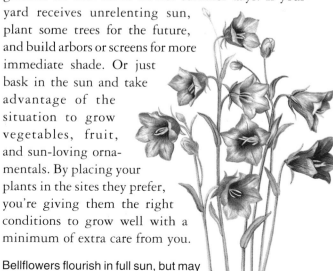

Sunny sites can provide ideal conditions for lush borders packed with light-loving, flowering perennials.

Bellflowers flourish in full sun, but may need shade in hot, sunny climates.

MOVING TOWARD LOW
MAINTENANCE

The definition of a low-maintenance landscape isn't the same for everyone. Maybe you hate mowing the lawn, but enjoy puttering in the flower garden. In that case, low maintenance would mean a small lawn so you have more time for plucking off spent blossoms. Or maybe you find mowing relaxing but hate trying to keep up with ripe vegetables that must be harvested. In that case, low maintenance might mean a tomato patch surrounded by an acre of turf.

The key to creating an attractive, easy-care landscape is deciding what you do and don't like to do and then planning your yard accordingly. Planning does require some time and effort, but it doesn't have to be a chore: You can spend a few minutes or hours as you have the chance and take as long as you want. Whether you're starting from scratch or modifying an existing landscape, you're most likely to get the results you want if you can envision how the project will look in the end and then create a realistic plan for getting there.

In this chapter, you'll learn how to come up with a personalized plan for your own easy-care landscape. "Creating a Low-maintenance Plan," on page 24, covers the basics of planning a layout that you can live with. "Starting from Scratch," on page 26, offers special pointers for creating a low-care landscape on an empty plot. If you want to reduce maintenance chores on an already-planted yard, see "Adapting an Existing Landscape," on page 27. In any case, you may have problem sites, like wet spots or rocky areas, that you just aren't sure how to deal with. The "Landscape Solutions Guide," starting on page 28, shows you low-maintenance options you can use to turn problem sites into pleasures.

Opposite: Hostas are a perfect choice for any low-maintenance garden that has a shady spot. They come in a wide variety of leaf shapes, colors, and sizes; many also have attractive flowers in summer.

Easy-care paths and plants like lady's mantles (*Alchemilla* spp.) are two elements of a low-maintenance garden.

Make the most of a small site with a combination of paving and low-care plants, like sedum and coneflowers.

Creating a Low-maintenance Plan

No matter what conditions you're starting with, the path to lower maintenance is easiest to follow when you have a map—not an actual road map, but rather a step-by-step plan that you've created to guide the transition from your existing yard to the easy-care landscape you've always wanted.

The process starts by taking a good, hard look at your whole yard, not just individual problem sites and high-maintenance areas. Developing an overall plan for your landscape will help you create a coherent, sensible design and avoid a piecemeal look. Once you have a plan, you can decide which areas get top priority based on your time and budget.

Make a Don't-wish List

Planning a low-maintenance landscape is more than just deciding what you *do* want; it's also important to know what you *don't* want. Take a realistic assessment of your landscape by grabbing a notebook and a pencil and strolling around your yard.

Jot down problem sites as you see them. Maybe it's that rocky patch in the backyard where nothing but weeds will grow. Or that steep grassy bank along the sidewalk that's a real pain to mow. Also look for high-maintenance elements that you may want to reduce or eliminate. Maybe you just can't stand the thought of clipping that endless privet hedge three times a year. Or perhaps you enjoy having some fresh produce, but are tired of tilling, weeding, and watering that huge vegetable garden every summer.

Add all of these notes to your "don't-wish" list. When you are finished, look back over the list and put a star next to the problems you'd like to deal with first. That will help you set priorities later on, when you begin to put together your plan for converting the existing landscape to low maintenance.

Sketch a Site Plan

After you've taken inventory of your yard's problem sites and high-maintenance areas, spend a few minutes drawing a rough sketch of the property. Mark the location of the house, garage, and any other structures, as well as the driveway, sidewalk, and other paved areas. Also note the location of existing large trees and shrubs, flower beds, and vegetable gardens. It doesn't have to be perfect—just good enough to help you visualize how things are laid out when you are indoors working on subsequent planning stages.

Try Your Options

Make a couple photocopies of your base plan, or lay sheets of tracing paper over the original sketch. On one copy or overlay, circle or otherwise mark the problem areas you identified on your stroll around the yard. On the other copies, try sketching in possible solutions. Maybe you could plant groundcovers on that grassy slope to eliminate mowing. Or link that group of shrubs with mulch and groundcovers, so you don't have to mow around the individual plants. If the vegetable garden is too big to take care of properly, how about reducing it to a few easy-to-maintain raised beds?

For more suggestions of low-maintenance landscape solutions, see "Starting from Scratch," on page 26, "Adapting an Existing Landscape," on page 27, and the "Landscape Solutions Guide," starting on page 28. Other chapters in this book offer even more ideas for reducing maintenance on lawns, trees and shrubs, flower gardens, and edible crops.

Experiment with different arrangements until you're happy with the results on paper. Then go out into the yard and try to visualize how the landscape will look with the solutions you've come up with. You may want to mark off each area with a rope to help you better imagine the layout. Think about how the whole yard will look viewed from different angles. Make sure you've planned for access by equipment (like mowers and wheelbarrows). Adjust the rough plan to match your new insights.

Draw a Detailed Plan

Once you like how the areas work together, draw a finished "solutions" plan to scale. It's handy to use a piece of graph paper. Choose a scale that will let you fit your whole property on one sheet of

Set Priority Projects

How you actually turn your solutions into reality depends on your time and budget. Don't try to convert the whole yard at one time—unless you have lots of time and lots of money. A better route is to set priority areas based on the most troublesome areas that you identified in the planning phase. Deal with the most time-consuming problems first, which will free up more time to tackle smaller changes in following years.

paper—such as 1 inch = 5 or 10 feet (2.5 cm = 1.5 or 3 m)—or use several sheets. Draw in the permanent features, like the house, garage, driveway, and deck. Also include any existing plants, as well as plants and features that you want to add. If you're not sure exactly what new plants you want, just draw in the space they'll take. Later you can pick specific plants adapted to the site.

Lawns

Reduce mowing chores by replacing some of the lawn with shrubs, trees, or groundcovers. Install mowing strips to cut down on edging chores (see "End Edging Forever" on page 43 for details). Make maintenance easier by eliminating grass growing under or along fences and walls, on steep slopes, and under low-branching or shallow-rooted trees.

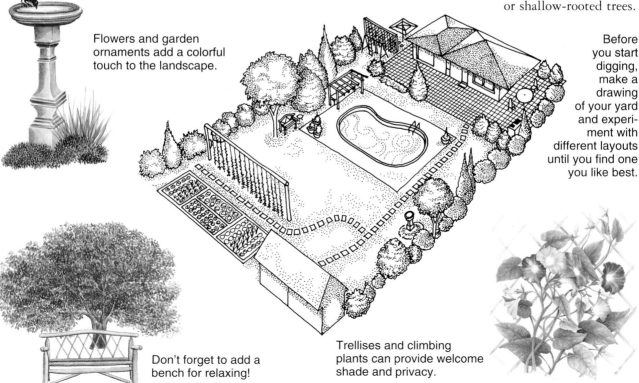

Flowers and garden ornaments add a colorful touch to the landscape.

Before you start digging, make a drawing of your yard and experiment with different layouts until you find one you like best.

Don't forget to add a bench for relaxing!

Trellises and climbing plants can provide welcome shade and privacy.

Add color to new gardens or fill in around developing shrubs and perennials with ageratums or other easy-care annuals.

Starting from Scratch

If you've just moved into a new development, built a new house, or inherited a particularly uninspired all-lawn landscape, you may be staring at bare soil or an expanse of grass where you want a garden to be located. Read through the sections below for tips on turning your blank lot into a beautiful, low-maintenance landscape.

Live with It

The best way to start a new landscape may be not to start it—at least for a year or so. If you can stand it, live with the landscape through 1 year. See where water puddles after storms or where it runs off quickly, taking valuable topsoil with it. Note where structures and trees cast shadows on your property throughout the seasons. See how traffic patterns develop: Where do you always walk to reach the car? Where do visitors and utility people tend to tread on their way to the door? Take note of these patterns and problems, and incorporate them into your landscape plan.

Plan for Easy-care Features

When you start a landscape from scratch, you can plan for low maintenance right from the start. Instead of high-maintenance hedges, provide privacy or block unsightly views with vine-covered fences or trellises. When laying out lawn areas, avoid sharp angles and curves that are hard to mow. Also, make sure that you leave plenty of room between planting beds to get mowers, tillers, and wheelbarrows in and out without running over plants. (A 12-inch [30 cm] path may be wide enough for you, but it's no match for an 18-inch [45 cm] wide mower!)

Pick Plants Carefully

As you choose plants for your new landscape, be sure to consider their growth rates and mature sizes. If you allow them enough room to develop without crowding the house or each other, you'll have healthier plants that need minimal pruning. If you're using foundation plantings, look for dwarf species and cultivars that won't grow up and block your view in a few years. Remember, the plants will look small when you put them in, but they'll grow surprisingly fast. If they look too awkward, plant annuals or perennials to fill in until the shrubs spread a bit.

Set Priorities

As you install your new landscape, it's wise to start on the "hard" elements—like walls, fences, and paths—first. This is also a good time to plan and install an automatic irrigation system if you need one. Once the permanent elements are in place, then you can start planting. Whenever possible, begin with slow growers like trees and shrubs, then the groundcovers. You may choose to plant a few beds of annuals for quick color during the first few seasons or to just wait for the perennial gardens to develop. Don't forget that annuals are also great for filling in gaps in young perennial gardens!

As you lay out your new garden, allow plenty of space between beds for easy access.

Adapting an Existing Landscape

In some ways, adapting an existing landscape is more challenging than starting from scratch. Although your yard may have nice features like large trees or an established lawn to work with, you also have someone else's mistakes to undo (or maybe your own, which are even harder to face).

If you've lived with the yard for at least a year, you are probably acutely aware of its troublesome or high-maintenance points. Don't try to convert the whole yard to low maintenance at once, though, or you may create more headaches than you solve. Identify the elements you want to change, and choose a few (or one major one) to work on each year. Below you'll find some pointers for handling specific areas. Also check out the following chapters for more suggestions: "Easy-care Lawns and Groundcovers," starting on page 40; "Timesaving Trees and Shrubs," starting on page 58; "Quick and Colorful Flower Gardens," starting on page 90; and "Effortless Edibles," starting on page 124.

Trees and Shrubs

Whenever possible, try to keep existing trees and shrubs. If the shrubs are overgrown, you might be able to give them a face-lift with drastic pruning (see "Shrubs That Take Severe Pruning" on page 67 for a list of shrubs that tolerate this treatment). If you do decide to remove a tree or shrub, make sure you dig out the stump, too—it's a lot of work, but it will make replanting much easier, and you won't have to deal with suckers sprouting from the roots.

If you are tired of pruning hedges, consider replacing these high-maintenance elements with informal shrub borders

Eliminate mowing under trees by replacing grass with groundcovers like common periwinkle (*Vinca minor*).

or with vine-covered fences or trellises. Or allow closely trimmed hedges to grow out some to soften into an equally attractive but more natural shape that needs less-frequent pruning.

Flowers

Many perennials are great for low-maintenance gardens. These fast-growing, adaptable plants can provide masses of seasonal color and beautiful foliage with just some basic care. If your existing plants are overgrown, dig them out, divide them, and replant the vigorous outer parts into enriched soil. If they are in the wrong spot, dig and move them in the spring.

If you don't mind the hassle of replanting them each year, annuals are great for season-long color. For lots of color without the hassle of digging flower beds, consider a few container plantings (if you're willing to do some extra watering).

Lawns

Reduce mowing chores by replacing some of the lawn with shrubs, trees, or groundcovers. Install mowing strips to cut down on edging chores (see "End Edging Forever" on page 43 for details). Make maintenance easier by eliminating grass growing under or along fences and walls, on steep slopes, and under any low-branching or shallow-rooted trees.

Minimize trimming around existing trees and shrubs by removing the sod around them and replacing it with mulch or groundcovers.

HOT, DRY SITES

Tamarisk's long-lasting flowers deliver color and fragrance under tough conditions. These trees even tolerate saline soils and seaside locations.

THE SOLUTION—SUITABLE PLANTS: Minimize the amount you have to water by landscaping with plants that are adapted to hot, dry conditions.

WILL IT WORK FOR YOU? Using plants that take arid conditions is a great solution for your climate.

WHAT TO DO: Look for plants with silvery leaves that can reflect excess sunlight or tap roots that can access water deep in the soil. Many succulents and aromatic herbs are also well adapted to heat and drought. Even with suitable plants, you'll have to take care to prepare a hospitable site. Water new plantings deeply until they develop enough roots to be self-supporting. Plan to water established plants during extensive droughts.

TREES: Cedars (*Cedrus* spp.), cypresses (*Cupressus* spp.), tamarisks (*Tamarix* spp.), palo verde (*Cercidium floridum*).

SHRUBS: Creeping juniper (*Juniperus horizontalis*), germander (*Teucrium fruticans*), eucalyptus (*Eucalyptus* spp.).

FLOWERS: Adam's-needle (*Yucca filamentosa*), yarrows (*Achillea* spp.), rose moss (*Portulaca grandiflora*), thrifts (*Armeria* spp.), wormwoods (*Artemisia* spp.), lamb's-ears (*Stachys byzantina*).

VEGETABLES AND HERBS: New Zealand spinach, Indian corn, pinto and tepary beans, thyme, sage, rosemary, lavender.

Drip irrigation puts water right where plants need it. Use it to grow vegetables in an inhospitable site, or hide it beneath a layer of mulch in a perennial border.

Organic mulches, such as bark chips, help keep the soil moist. As they break down, such mulches add organic matter to the soil, improving its moisture-holding capacity.

THE SOLUTION—DRIP IRRIGATION: Use drip irrigation to help drought-tolerant plants get started or to maintain plants that need more water. Drip irrigation releases water at soil level to targeted areas; little water evaporates or is wasted on uncultivated space. Drip irrigation also minimizes the spread of diseases, since plant leaves stay dry.

WILL IT WORK FOR YOU? Absolutely, although you need to find the drip system that suits your needs. Permanent systems made of plastic tubing take money and engineering to install but do their job with the flick of a switch. Temporary, inexpensive soaker hoses can be moved around as necessary. Be sure that you irrigate thoroughly each time you water, so plant roots will grow deep and be better able to scavenge moisture.

WHAT TO DO: Make a simple system yourself. Buy a drip irrigation kit with supply lines, valves, and fittings. Run the lines up and down garden rows or make a network of lines through free-form gardens. Carefully choose where you insert the emitters (the parts that release a trickle of water). Place them where they'll wet the entire rooting area of each plant or moisten the entire row, wide bed, or cultivated area; otherwise roots may stay concentrated right near the emitters. Consult an irrigation supplier to have a drip irrigation system custom-tailored to your landscape.

THE SOLUTION—GROWING TECHNIQUES: Plant in a naturally moist low spot or dig sunken beds. Make a small, moisture-holding well around each new plant. Shade your garden with trees or trellises. Add organic matter and mulch to the soil. Group plants with similar water needs; separate those that need irrigation from those that don't.

WILL IT WORK FOR YOU? Any of these techniques, and especially combinations of them, can make plants grow better with less effort on your part.

WHAT TO DO: Dig sunken beds 2–4 inches (5–10 cm) deep and 8–48 inches (20–120 cm) wide for vegetable gardens. In ornamental plantings, make a lower level in the front of the bed for low-growing plants that need more moisture.

Dig a water-catching basin 2 inches (5 cm) deep and slightly wider than the root ball around new plantings. Fill it in once plants are established.

To block the late afternoon sun and moderate midsummer's most intense heat, plant a shade-casting tree or a large shrub northwest of your garden or patio. For quick shade, grow a deciduous vine over a lath structure or trellis.

Cover the garden with 4–6 inches (10–15 cm) of an organic mulch like compost or bark chips to reduce water loss by 70 percent. If you use fine-textured mulches like dried grass clippings, make the layers thinner so they don't stop air flow.

A combination of steps and terraced beds turns this steep slope from a maintenance problem into a delightful garden that can be tended with ease.

Low-growing, spreading perennial flowers, like these moss pinks, are both attractive and functional when used to prevent erosion on gently sloping sites.

THE SOLUTION—TERRACED BEDS: Create level planting areas and hold them in place with retaining walls of wattling, stone, timbers, or brick.

WILL IT WORK FOR YOU? On gentle slopes, you can build terraces yourself or plant without terracing. When a slope is severe, terracing may be the only way to keep plants and soil from washing away. However, this kind of construction project takes time, effort, and expense, factors that grow proportionately with the steepness of the slope, so you may need professional help.

WHAT TO DO: Dig out level planting areas on the slope. If using stone retaining walls, angle the walls with a receding upward slope to handle the soil pressure. If you mortar the structure, leave small openings for excess water to drain through.

Make natural-looking wattling retaining walls with bundles of green twigs from woody plants that root and sucker easily. These include willows (*Salix* spp.), sumacs (*Rhus* spp.), and common lilac (*Syringa vulgaris*). Tie the twigs together in bundles 6–10 inches (15–25 cm) wide and 2–3 feet (60–90 cm) long. Taper the bundles on each end. Overlay the tapered ends of adjoining bundles to form the retaining wall. Hold the bundles in place with wooden or metal stakes. Fill in behind the bundles with soil. If desired, also cover the bundles with soil. In time, they may begin to grow.

THE SOLUTION—SUITABLE PLANTS: Cover a gentle slope with grass or spreading groundcovers or shrubs. Once rooted, they can prevent erosion.

WILL IT WORK FOR YOU? This works well if the slope is not too steep. Plant lawn only if the slope is less than a 10-percent grade. For grades of 10 to 25 percent, cover the slope with groundcovers or spreading shrubs.

WHAT TO DO: Sow grass seed and cover it with biodegradable burlap to keep it in place until it germinates. To get groundcovers started on a slope, carve out a flat planting area with raised edges. Set the plant close to the outer edge; the inner part will fill in with soil carried down from farther up the slope. The pocket will eventually disappear, but usually not before the plant is securely anchored. Use drip irrigation to keep the area moist until the new plants are established. Listed below are some excellent plants for sloping sites:

SHRUBS: Border forsythia (*Forsythia* x *intermedia*), creeping juniper (*Juniperus horizontalis*), sumacs (*Rhus* spp.), rugosa rose (*Rosa rugosa*), willows (*Salix* spp.), common lilac (*Syringa vulgaris*), or lace shrub (*Stephanandra incisa*).

GROUNDCOVERS: Periwinkles (*Vinca spp.*) or English ivy (*Hedera helix*).

PERENNIALS: Daylilies (*Hemerocallis* spp.) or moss pink (*Phlox subulata*).

Barriers can reduce wind velocity for distances up to five times their height; for example, a 6-foot (1.8 m) fence would provide a 30-foot (9 m) wind block.

Sturdy rugosa roses grow and thrive in sites too windy for many plants. Enjoy their flowers and bright orange hips and grow more delicate plants in their shelter.

THE SOLUTION—HEDGES AND FENCES: Plant a hedge or install a fence to block the wind.

WILL IT WORK FOR YOU? Hedges take time to grow and need space to spread, occasional fertilizing, and water (which might be a problem in dry locations). You also may have to prune to keep the foliage dense enough to block wind.

A fence takes less space than a hedge but can cost more to install. A fence to the south, east, or west of your yard will cast a permanent shadow that can create shade problems. If the fence faces south, the sun's reflection may create a warm pocket in the garden, which can be handy in cool areas but less desirable in hot ones.

WHAT TO DO: First, check with your local zoning board for any restrictions on fence or hedge heights.

You can build your own 2-foot (60 cm) high wall of stone or brick, but call in a professional for taller walls. Wood is less expensive, but if you need a professional to build the fence, the price will go up.

Formal hedges are attractive but need regular trimming. For less work, try an informal hedge. Space the shrubs so they can grow to 90 percent of their full spread, letting their branch tips intermingle to make a solid wall of vegetation.

THE SOLUTION—SUITABLE PLANTS: Use tough, strong-stemmed plants that can take some wind.

WILL IT WORK FOR YOU? Choosing appropriate plants for windy locations will help ensure that what you plant can survive with minimal care. If winds are too strong, consider also making a wind break (see "Hedges and Fences").

WHAT TO DO: Use taller, wind-tolerant plants at the perimeter of your yard or garden to cut wind velocity and shelter other plants. Grow dwarf or low-growing species or cultivars that are less likely to be blown down; stake taller flowers. Prepare a moisture-retentive soil, and mulch with a coarse, dust-free material, such as bark chips, that won't blow in the wind. Because plants exposed to wind dry out faster, be sure to irrigate in dry weather.

Wind-tolerant species include the following:
TREES: Tamarisks (*Tamarix* spp.), mesquite (*Prosapis glandulosa*), golden rain tree (*Koelreuteria paniculata*), limber pine (*Pinus flexilis*).
SHRUBS: Barberries (*Berberis* spp.), rugosa rose (*Rosa rugosa*), rockspray cotoneaster (*Cotoneaster horizontalis*).
PERENNIALS: Dwarf asters (*Aster* spp.), lance-leaved coreopsis (*Coreopsis lanceolata*), daylilies (*Hemerocallis* spp.), thrifts (*Armeria* spp.), stonecrops (*Sedum* spp.), moss pink (*Phlox subulata*), begonias, marigolds, petunias.

ROCKY AREAS

Use the rocks you find in your landscape as the framework for a raised rock garden. Mound topsoil over and amid the rocks and plant in the crevices and pockets between them.

THE SOLUTION—RAISED BEDS: If your landscape is riddled with small rocks, you can dig them out and save them for stone walls or terraces. For an easy alternative, mound rock-free topsoil over or amid rocks, making a well-drained bed suitable for shallow-rooted plants.

WILL IT WORK FOR YOU? Moving rocks is hard work. Gardening over them may be an easier option, but it will limit your plant choices. Choose species (such as those under "Suitable Plants") that tolerate limited rooting room and well-drained soil.

WHAT TO DO: Raise a bed about 12 inches (30 cm) above existing rocks to plant shallow-rooted species. Or leave the top third of the rock exposed to create an alpine garden. Make layers of stone that resemble a rock outcropping. Set similar-looking, long rectangular stones into a mound of humus-rich soil. Lay them horizontally with the broadest part of the rock flat on the soil. Slope the back of the rock downward so moisture runs off it into the soil behind. Let rectangular rocks rise like mountain peaks between the outcroppings. Plant in the crevices and pockets between the rocks. Use dwarf bulbs and conifers, small deep-rooted plants, alpine plants native to mountain tops, or other hardy low-growing plants.

Rocky sites need not be barren ones. Enjoy the color provided by mounded, creeping, or cascading plants that tolerate shallow, well-drained soils.

THE SOLUTION—SUITABLE PLANTS: Low, mounded, creeping, or cascading plants are natural companions for rocky areas.

WILL IT WORK FOR YOU? If you spend some time finding suitable plants, you will be rewarded with an unusual and interesting garden. If they are not available locally, you can order them by mail.

WHAT TO DO: Look for suitable plants that are adapted to your garden's light and soil conditions. Work young plants into loose soil, then firm the soil well so it won't wash away. Water gently and deeply until plants become established.

Here are some species you can try:

TREES : Dwarf weeping hemlock (*Tsuga canadensis* 'Pendula Nana'), Japanese maple (*Acer palmatum*), dwarf spruces (*Picea* spp.), dwarf firs (*Abies* spp.).

SHRUBS: Dwarf rhododendrons and azaleas (*Rhododendron* spp.), creeping juniper (*Juniperus horizontalis*), dwarf conifers.

FLOWERS: Lady's-mantles (*Alchemilla* spp.), violets (*Viola* spp.), cranesbills (*Geranium* spp.), California poppy (*Eschscholzia californica*), Carpathian harebell (*Campanula carpatica*), maiden pinks (*Dianthus deltoides*), alpine bellflower (*Campanula alpina*), pasque flower (*Anemone pulsatilla*), common thrift (*Armeria maritima*), alpine aster (*Aster alpinus*), cyclamen (*Cyclamen* spp.).

EDIBLES: Alpine strawberries, creeping thyme.

SEASIDE GARDENS

If planted in a sheltered location, a number of landscape plants, including versatile junipers, can withstand windy seaside conditions and sandy soil.

THE SOLUTION—SUITABLE PLANTS: Many attractive plants grow naturally in the salt spray, winds, and sandy soil of seaside climates.

WILL IT WORK FOR YOU? In exposed, oceanside locations, you will not be able to grow anything but durable, well-adapted plants. If you are slightly inland or can create a sheltered planting site, you may be able to grow a wider range of plants.

WHAT TO DO: Choose plants for exposed and protected locations from the list below and consult "Growing Techniques" for tips on growing them successfully.

OCEANSIDE LOCATIONS: Check local regulations about oceanside plantings and look for durable species, such as Russian olive (*Elaeagnus angustifolia*), Japanese black pine (*Pinus thunbergiana*), beach plum (*Prunus maritima*), rugosa rose (*Rosa rugosa*), bearberry (*Arctostaphylos uva-ursi*), broom (*Cytisus decumbens*), sea oats (*Uniola paniculata*), American beach grass (*Ammophila breviligulata*), and broomsedge (*Andropogon virginicus*).

PROTECTED GARDEN SITES: Northern bayberry (*Myrica pensylvanica*), junipers (*Juniperus* spp.), common thrift (*Ameria maritima*), rock cresses (*Arabis* spp.), sea holly (*Eryngium maritimum*), sedums (*Sedum* spp.), California poppy (*Eschscholzia californica*), cornflower (*Centaurea cyanus*), beach pea (*Lathyrus littoralis*), sun roses (*Helianthemum* spp.).

Create a screen of extra-durable plants to shield a seaside planting from wind and salt spray. Amend the soil and mulch with organic matter to help plants take hold.

THE SOLUTION—GROWING TECHNIQUES: Screens and soil improvements are easy ways to ensure successful gardening.

WILL IT WORK FOR YOU? Successful planting near the seashore takes a lot of preparation and planning. How you proceed will depend on the natural topography, view, and prevailing winds. Evaluate what kind of difficulties the site creates for plant growth so you can moderate them. Wind blowing off the sea will carry salt spray that can burn plants. Decide if you can block the wind with a fence or screen. This makes a hidden garden nook—a sheltered site with improved growing conditions. Or accent the view of your surroundings using salt-tolerant plants.

WHAT TO DO: Moderate dry, nutrient-poor, sandy soil by adding organic matter before planting and mulching after planting. If you have a dramatic overlook of the ocean, preserve it by planting low plants. If you want to create a protected garden, plant a screen of extra-durable plants to hold back shifting beach sand and to cut the wind. (See "Suitable Plants" for suggestions.) Screen out some of the wind and salt temporarily to get young trees started by setting snow fencing or brush about 5 feet (1.5 m) in front of each plant. Once the plant is well rooted and growing, remove the screen.

Willows (Salix spp.) happily inhabit soggy soils and water-side sites too wet for many other plants. Combine them with water-loving blue or yellow flags.

Build raised beds to turn a wet site into a well-drained garden. Simply rake the soil into 4–6-inch (10–15 cm) mounds, or frame beds with timbers, stone, or brick.

THE SOLUTION—SUITABLE PLANTS: Grow a variety of plants that thrive in moist or wet soil.

WILL IT WORK FOR YOU? Creating a garden with moisture-tolerant plants is a relatively inexpensive solution for this type of problem.

WHAT TO DO: Many plants are adapted to moist sites with occasional standing water. Some of the best are listed below.

PLANTS FOR DAMP SOILS: If the area is damp year-round, but not underwater, choose plants that prefer abundant moisture.

Trees: Dawn redwood (*Metasequoia glyptostroboides*), tupelos (*Nyssa* spp.), red maple (*Acer rubrum*).

Shrubs: Pussy willow (*Salix discolor*), red-osier dogwood (*Cornus sericea*), winterberry (*Ilex verticillata*).

Perennials: Astilbes (*Astilbe* spp.), common sneezeweed (*Helenium autumnale*), Joe-Pye weed (*Eupatorium purpureum*), cardinal flower (*Lobelia cardinalis*).

MARSH PLANTS FOR STANDING WATER: If your site has 3–6 inches (7.5–15 cm) of standing water year-round, try marsh plants. (If your water is deeper than this, a pond may be a more practical solution.)

Trees: Bald cypress (*Taxodium distichum*).

Perennials: Blue flag (*Iris versicolor*), yellow flag (*Iris pseudacorus*), arrowhead (*Sagittaria* spp.), pickerel weed (*Pontederia cordata*).

THE SOLUTION—RAISED BEDS: Raised beds can provide enough well-drained surface soil for shallow-rooted plants like most flowers and vegetables.

WILL IT WORK FOR YOU? Raised beds—especially when enclosed in low frames or retaining walls—provide a long-term solution for wet spots, so they are well worth the effort to build.

In warm climates, raised beds can dry out quickly, so you may want to build beds no more than 4 inches (10 cm) tall. To help keep raised beds cool and moist, make the raised part out of moisture-holding soil such as a clay loam or topsoil enriched with organic matter. In cool climates, beds are usually 6–8 inches (15–20 cm) deep.

WHAT TO DO: Rake topsoil into temporary mounds in the vegetable garden, or build permanent beds and frame them with rot-resistant landscape timbers or 2 x 10 (roughly 5 x 25 cm) lumber. Hold the wood together with brackets and anchor it in place with stakes.

To build a dry stone retaining wall, use flat stones that are 1–2 feet (30–60 cm) wide. Center each stone over the junction between two stones below. Fill in between and behind them with soil.

Build a low, mortared brick retaining wall set on a 6-inch (15 cm) deep cement or sand footer. If you need a wall over 2 feet (60 cm) tall, consult a professional landscaper or builder.

Diverting excess water into a pond or retaining basin can add an attractive feature to your landscape while controlling moisture problems in the rest of the yard.

Double-digging to a depth of 18 inches (45 cm) breaks up compacted soil layers that trap moisture near the surface. Add organic matter to further loosen heavy soils.

THE SOLUTION—DRAINAGE TECHNIQUES: Even if most of your yard is wet, you can solve the problem by installing a drainage system or by diverting water downhill into a pond or retaining basin. If you are planning large-scale drainage alterations, consult a contractor before you go ahead—there may be legal concerns regarding water flow on your property.

WILL IT WORK FOR YOU? Consider all the alternatives to find the solution that's right for you.

WHAT TO DO: If your yard slopes, you can capture excess rainfall in a low part of your yard. If the area floods occasionally, make the low area a turf-covered retaining basin that you can treat like lawn when it dries out. If the soil in this area stays wet or slightly underwater all year long, make it a swale planted with water-loving species (see "Suitable Plants"). This can turn a problem area into a beautiful garden of unusual plants.

If the low area holds a foot or more of water, you can excavate down about 3 feet (90 cm) and turn it into a pond. Line the bottom with plastic and add waterlilies, oxygenating plants (which grow underwater and give off oxygen), and fish.

Underground drainage tiles are a permanent solution to widespread wet conditions. However, they are expensive and hard to install; consider hiring a professional.

THE SOLUTION—GROWING TECHNIQUES: Loosen heavy soils with organic matter. Raise planting areas by 2–4 inches (5–10 cm) to keep the crown dry on plants like blueberries and rhododendrons; they like access to moist soil but not immersion in it. Double dig 18 inches (45 cm) deep to break up compacted lower soil layers that may trap moisture near the surface.

WILL IT WORK FOR YOU? All options involve some work but can be effective.

WHAT TO DO: To amend the soil in heavy clay areas, work in 1–2 inches (2.5–5 cm) of well-decayed leaf mold, compost, or rotted livestock manure. To replace what has decayed, mulch each year with 1 inch (2.5 cm) of organic matter (even more in hot climates).

Raise the planting area to dry out heavy soil and areas that are only occasionally wet before planting. See "Raised Beds" for information on building temporary and permanent beds.

To double dig compacted soil, remove a spade-deep strip of topsoil from the area and place it in a wheelbarrow. Use a garden fork or spade to loosen the soil below. Dig another strip of topsoil from beside the first and move it over to the first trench. Loosen the exposed lower layer of soil. Continue until you reach the last strip. Fill it with the topsoil from the wheelbarrow.

SHADY SITES

Jewel-like impatiens will thrive even in deep shade if the soil is rich and evenly moist. Few plants fare well in dry shade beneath shallow- or thickly rotted trees.

Durable daylilies are equally at home in sun or light shade. Their ability to withstand dry soils makes them ideal for planting at the edge of a wooded area.

THE SOLUTION—SUITABLE PLANTS: Fill the spot with some of the many flowering and foliage plants that grow well in shade.

WILL IT WORK FOR YOU? Choose plants adapted to your yard's particular conditions. Gardens on the north side of a house, in coniferous woods, or under mature shade trees are usually in deep shade. Little sunlight reaches the ground and few flowers or shrubs grow. You can cultivate durable groundcovers or simply spread a carpet of mulch.

In medium shade, some sunlight reaches the ground through the tree canopy. Lightly shaded areas on the east or west side of the house or the edge of the woods receive about a half day of sun. If root competition is not too severe, you can plant flowers and shrubs that make do with a couple hours of sunlight.

When you are selecting species for shade, consider soil moisture, too. Under shallow or thickly rooted trees, like Norway and silver maples (*Acer platanoides* and *A. saccharinum*) and beeches (*Fagus* spp.), the soil may be parchingly dry. Fewer plants will grow there. Many more species will grow in moist, shady sites.

WHAT TO DO: If the soil is dry or riddled with roots, amend the planting area with plenty of organic matter (see "Growing Techniques"). Water and fertilize more often to prevent plants competing for limited resources. In very dry sites where plants just won't grow well, substitute bark or stone mulch.

In moist soil in light shade, try azaleas and rhododendrons (*Rhododendron* spp.), laurels (*Kalmia* spp.), oak-leaved hydrangea (*Hydrangea quercifolia*), astilbes (*Astilbe* spp.), and impatiens.

In dry soil and light shade, try burning bush (*Euonymus alata*), Japanese kerria (*Kerria japonica*), and daylilies (*Hemerocallis* spp.).

In medium shade, take advantage of early spring before the trees leaf out. Plant spring-flowering bulbs, wildflowers, and perennials such as bleeding hearts (*Dicentra* spp.), and squills (*Scilla* spp.).

In fairly dry sites, you can fill out the rest of the growing season with epimediums (*Epimedium* spp.), Japanese painted fern (*Athyrium goeringianum* 'Pictum'), and Western polypody (*Polypodium hesperium*). In moist sites, try summersweet (*Clethra alnifolia*), Oregon grape (*Mahonia aquifolium*), astilbes (*Astilbe* spp.), ostrich fern (*Matteuccia struthiopteris*), royal fern (*Osmunda regalis*), hostas (*Hosta* spp.), hellebores (*Helleborus* spp.), primroses (*Primula* spp.), sweet woodruff (*Galium odoratum*), and tuberous begonias.

In deep shade, grow extra-durable plants like ivy (*Hedera helix*), pachysandra (*Pachysandra terminalis*), and periwinkle (*Vinca major*).

To give your shade garden a strong start, thin out branches to admit more light, amend and mulch the soil, and plant close to tree trunks where few feeder roots grow.

THE SOLUTION—GROWING TECHNIQUES: To lighten shade and reduce root competition, thin out tree canopies or remove lower tree limbs to let more sunlight through. Plant close to tree trunks, where feeding roots aren't active. Amend and mulch planting areas so they will hold more moisture and nutrients. Plant small plants; they adapt more quickly to shade and need smaller planting holes.

WILL IT WORK FOR YOU? Try a combination of these methods to get the best results. For your safety, hire professionals to prune large trees.

WHAT TO DO: To deal with root-riddled planting areas, make planting pockets. When you plant a shrub, make the hole extra wide and clear out all roots under 1 inch (2.5 cm) in diameter. Or plant small plants close to the tree trunk where you can find patches of open soil between the large tree roots. Dig down to loosen the soil and plant.

After planting, surround the new plant with a shallow soil basin. Let water from a hose trickle gently into it whenever the soil becomes dry until the plant becomes established.

To improve the soil, add a 1-inch (2.5 cm) layer of compost to planting areas or use it as a mulch over existing plantings. Or you can substitute 3–4-inch (7.5–10 cm) layers of coarse wood chips or shredded leaves mixed with straw.

Architectural features, such as patios, benches, rocks, or fallen logs, add year-round interest to a shady site and don't compete with trees for water and nutrients.

THE SOLUTION—DESIGN CONSIDERATIONS: Use your shady yard as an outdoor living area for relaxing in summer. Put in a deck or patio in a dry, shady spot. Or turn a shady tree grove into a woodland garden. Use plants with white or light yellow flowers or variegated leaves to brighten the shade. Let your container-grown flowers and vegetables grow in the comfort of light shade in midsummer.

WILL IT WORK FOR YOU? Decks and patios are expensive to install but will give you years of pleasure. Woodland gardens can be lively in spring when you're aching for color and in the fall when the leaves change color. They also harbor an interesting array of wildlife—some of which (such as deer and rabbits) may become garden pests.

WHAT TO DO: To brighten woodland gardens, plant light-colored flowers, spring-blooming wildflowers, and perennials with variegated leaves such as hostas (*Hostas* spp.). (See "Suitable Plants" for more ideas.)

You can build a wooden deck or make a patio on the ground of brick, stone, or paving tiles. However, surface-rooting trees, such as Norway or silver maples (*Acer platanoides* or *A. saccharinum*), may buckle in-ground patios. Save yourself this agony by making a sitting area of mulch or gravel under these trees.

Edging materials can help define plantings while keeping grass out and spreading plants in. Shape beds with gentle curves and straight lines for easier installation.

A strip of bricks, set into the soil around a bed, lets you mow right up to the edge of the planting, eliminating time-consuming trimming chores.

THE SOLUTION—EDGING MATERIALS: You can keep grass out of your garden beds, and aggressive groundcovers out of your lawn, by edging beds with a root barrier. This simple procedure will save you much trimming, edging, and weeding.

WILL IT WORK FOR YOU? For the least maintenance, look for a durable edging material that will stay in place for many years. Some plastic or fiberglass strips tend to sink down or work up and lose their effectiveness. Metal, wood, or stone can be more stable. It's not difficult to install edgings, but you need time and patience to do it right. Set the edging high enough so grasses can't creep over it but low enough so it won't interfere with your lawn mower.

WHAT TO DO: Begin by making a clean, smooth line around the bed to show you where to put the edging. Pull a string taut between two stakes to mark straight areas and use a curved garden hose for the rounded lines. Then choose the edging technique that will work best for you.

TRENCHING: Dig a shallow trench about 1 inch (2.5 cm) wide around your garden beds. Keep the trench free of vegetation. Go over it with a string trimmer or hoe every week or two during the growing season.

BARRIER STRIPS: Block root growth with a vertical barrier like a 1-inch (2.5 cm) thick, 6-inch (15 cm) wide cedar board. To install it, use a flat spade to make a straight-sided trench around the bed. Dig the trench about 7 inches (17.5 cm) deep and put 2 inches (5 cm) of coarse builders' sand in the bottom. Work the boards down into the sand so that about ½ inch (12 mm) of the wood emerges. Keep boards in place by driving ½-inch (12 mm) steel spikes into the ground beside the boards every 18 inches (45 cm). You also can buy rubber, fiberglass, and metal edgings that work as barriers.

LANDSCAPE TIMBERS: Set 4 x 4 (roughly 10 x 10 cm) landscape timbers on about 1 inch (2.5 cm) of sand, so their surface is even with or up to ¼ inch (6 mm) higher than the surrounding soil. Drive spikes through both ends to keep them in place.

BRICK: Set bricks vertically on a sand base in a trench, or lay them horizontally, side by side, on a cement footer for a wider decorative edging. Don't let the top of the bricks emerge more than about ½ inch (12 mm) higher than the bed, so you can mow over them.

STONE: Lay flagstones side by side in a shallow sand trench for some edging benefits. Set one line of rocks below the soil surface and a top layer even with the soil. Unless you set the stones in cement, though, some grass or weed roots eventually will work through the openings between the stones.

A flagstone path admits visitors to the heart of a cottage garden. Low-growing plants between the paving soften the path's edges and make it a part of the garden.

Choose paving materials that suit your garden's style and your budget. An inexpensive wood chip path fits in nicely in an informal woodland garden.

THE SOLUTION—PATHS AND WALKWAYS: Add elegance and accessibility to your landscape with paths or walkways. Paths can be an attractive feature of your garden as well as make it easier to get around. Use a walkway to let you into a large garden so you can maintain it without trampling plants. Let a walkway divide the rooting zone of a hedge from a garden bed planted next to it.

WILL IT WORK FOR YOU? You need to find a paving material that will look good, be functional, and fit in your budget. The paving material should match or complement the style or color of your existing landscape or home. For example, a brick wall looks great with a brick home. A stone walk complements a country cottage. The paving material you choose also should be easy to maintain. Although they are expensive to buy, paving block, stone, and brick require little additional maintenance after they are installed.

WHAT TO DO: Design the path or walkway on paper before you build it. Make it wide enough so that it is easy to use. A walk to your door should be 4 feet (1.2 m) wide, spacious enough to accommodate two people walking side by side. You can make a utility path in the garden 2 feet (60 cm) wide. Make sure your walk is well drained so you can use it during wet weather and so it won't shift and jar as the soil freezes and thaws. For a paved path,

excavate 6–8 inches (15–20 cm) deep. Line the exposed soil with 2–4 inches (5–10 cm) of ground rock and firm it well. Top the ground rock with a 1–3-inch (2.5–7.5 cm) layer of coarse builders' sand. Lay the flagstone, brick, or paving block on the sand; fill in any gaps with more sand.

If you want an inexpensive path, choose loose surfaces like gravel and wood chips, but remember that they need regular replacement and are difficult to set furniture on. To use wood chips for a walk, strip off the turf and cover with a 4-inch (10 cm) layer of wood chips. For a gravel walk, dig down 2–4 inches (5–10 cm) and edge the walk with landscape timbers, rocks, or brick. Fill the remaining low area with gravel. You'll have to replace wood chips and gravel once or twice a year when the walk begins to get low. Plan to weed or rake the path occasionally to eliminate weeds. Or lay a fabric weed barrier under the gravel or wood chips to minimize weed growth.

EASY-CARE LAWNS AND GROUNDCOVERS

Lawn maintenance is probably the most routine and time-consuming part of caring for a traditional landscape. If you're one of those people who find mowing a relaxing, meditative task, your ideal low-maintenance landscape may be mostly an expanse of unbroken lawn. But even then, you may want to reduce related lawn-care chores, like hand-trimming edges along beds and paths. The rest of us welcome *any* technique that lets us spend less time mowing, trimming, weeding, fertilizing, and watering that plot of grass.

How much time you end up devoting to your lawn depends on how manicured a look you want. Obviously, your summers will be more leisurely if you only mow when you have to and don't bother fertilizing, watering, or weeding. If your lawn is in good shape and you don't have a drought, the odds are good that you can get away with this approach and still have a normal-looking yard.

If you have a lawn that's in bad shape, it may take a few years of effort before it looks good and requires little maintenance. To bring back a neglected lawn, you can overseed with improved grass cultivars (see "Picking the Perfect Grass" on page 42 for tips on selecting the best kinds for your yard). Apply compost or a lawn-restoring fertilizer that adds microorganisms to the soil. Water during dry spells, and pull weeds before they set seed. Restoring a neglected lawn can be an ordeal. But once it's back in shape, you can keep it up with a simple care program.

In this chapter, you'll learn the basics for establishing a healthy lawn that will be naturally less prone to problems. "Creating a Low-maintenance Lawn" on page 42 helps you choose the best grasses for your conditions and tells you how to start a new lawn or renovate your existing yard. Once your lawn is in good shape, follow the information in "Easy Lawn Care" on page 44 to keep the yard looking great without slaving over it every weekend. If you'd like to have less lawn overall, check out "Reducing Lawn Area" on page 46 for information on replacing some or all of the lawn with mulches, wildflowers, or groundcovers.

Opposite: Groundcovers are a great solution for tough-to-mow spots, especially around trees and shrubs. Combine several different groundcover plants—like bergenias (*Bergenia* spp.) and English ivy—for a tapestry effect.

Creating a Low-maintenance Lawn

The kind of grass you grow has a lot to do with how much maintenance it requires. Although your choices are limited by where in the country you live and what is available at local garden centers and nurseries, some lawn grasses you can grow are lower maintenance than others. Picking the right grasses, and planting them properly, will go a long way toward creating a great-looking, easy-care lawn.

Picking the Perfect Grass

Start your search for the right lawn grass by considering your climate. Grasses fall into two basic groups: cool-season species and warm-season species. Cool-season grasses, such as Kentucky bluegrass and the fescues, turn green in the spring, then go dormant and turn brown in the summer unless you water them regularly. Warm-season grasses, like bermudagrass and St. Augustine grass, don't green up until daytime temperatures climb to about 80°F (25°C) and nighttime temperatures reach about 60°F (15°C).

Starting with grass species that are adapted to your area will help ensure a healthy, beautiful lawn.

If you garden in the North, look for cool-season grasses. In the South, warm-season grasses are the obvious choice. In moderate-climate, transitional areas, lawns may contain either type.

As you consider the grasses that will grow in your climate, look for ones that suit your growing conditions and your lifestyle. Grasses vary in the amount of light they require; some need full sun while others tolerate shade. Certain species need more water (possibly requiring extra irrigation); some grow more slowly than others (meaning less frequent mowing). Tougher grasses hold up to foot traffic; others fade away with frequent trampling. Additional factors to consider include how fast the grass grows and how resistant it is to pests and diseases. Knowledgeable garden center staff can advise you on the most current choices for your conditions. Your local Cooperative Extension Service can also provide advice on finding the right grasses.

Mixing It Up

Because grasses vary widely in their characteristics and adaptability, it's common for Northern gardeners to

---

Renovating an Existing Lawn

If your existing lawn is basically healthy, you may just want to renovate it by overseeding. Pick a cool, moist time of year—early spring or fall—to get the new seed off to a good start.

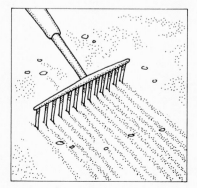

Mow the area closely, and rake vigorously to scratch the soil surface.

Sow seed over the area; cover with a ½-inch (1 cm) layer of compost.

Roll lightly to get good contact between the seeds, soil, and compost.

Choose red fescue for sites that get some shade. Leave it unmowed for a meadow-like appearance in informal areas.

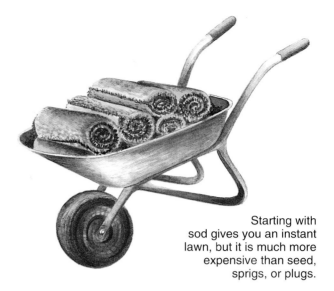

Starting with sod gives you an instant lawn, but it is much more expensive than seed, sprigs, or plugs.

plant a lawn that's a mixture of a few grass species. If you have some shady areas, for example, you might plant a mix of sun-loving Kentucky bluegrass and more shade-tolerant red fescue. (Species mixes are less popular in the South because the commonly grown grasses are so competitive and the textures of the leaves clash.)

Mixes can also contain several cultivars of the same species. Within each grass species, cultivars vary in their shade tolerance and disease and insect resistance. Planting a mix, rather than a single cultivar, creates a lawn that adapts to dry years and wet years, sunny areas and shady spots. Because new cultivars make it to market regularly, you should call your local Cooperative Extension Service for its current recommendations.

Starting a New Lawn

If you want a completely new lawn, you can start it from seed, sod, sprigs, or plugs. Seed is the least expensive, but it takes the longest to establish and may require frequent sprinkling during germination. Sod is expensive but gives an instant lawn. Sprigs are individual rooted grass plants; plugs are small pieces of sod planted about 1 foot (30 cm) apart. They're less expensive than sod and establish faster than seed.

No matter what method you choose, you'll get the best results if you prepare the site well. Strip off any existing sod, and loosen the soil to a depth of at least 4 inches (10 cm). If your site has very poor soil, you may want to add some new topsoil. As you prepare the soil, work in a ½-inch (1 cm) layer of compost to add nutrients and organic matter. Rake to smooth the soil surface; then sow the seed or lay the sod strips. Keep the area evenly moist until the seeds germinate or the sod pieces start to grow together.

End Edging Forever

For the busy gardener, trees, shrubs, and flower beds can quickly turn from a triumph to a trial. The shaggy edges that form between plantings and lawn areas can give any landscape an unkempt look, and they're a real pain to trim.

Mowing strips are the solution. A mowing strip is a flat band, usually of brick or cut rock, that sits flush with the soil and

edges flower beds and no-mow zones around trees. (Easy-to-install commercial plastic edgings are also available.) Rather than using hand or string trimmers to cut the grass at the edge of the bed, you just mow it, letting one wheel ride the strip and the other the lawn.

To install a mowing strip, dig a shallow trench the width of edging material along the edge of the bed. Set the edging snugly in the trench, so it's slightly below the level of the lawn. If you're using brick or rock and your soil is a clay that shrinks and swells, make a deeper trench and fill it with 1 to 2 inches (2.5 to 5 cm) of sand. Level the sand before setting in the bricks or rocks.

Easy Lawn Care

It's Saturday, so it must be time to pull out that wretched mower and chase it across the yard for a few hours, right? Not necessarily, if you have a low-maintenance lawn. Mowing only when the lawn needs it, rather than on a set schedule, can free up many summer weekends and give you healthier turf to boot. Sensible watering and fertilizing routines also help reduce maintenance chores while promoting a naturally problem-resistant lawn.

Mowing

Many gardeners keep their grass much shorter than necessary. Let your grass grow to its ideal height—instead of cutting it every week whether it needs it or not—and you'll probably spend less time pushing a mower around. The optimal height varies with the species; "Ideal Grass Heights" gives you guidelines for many common lawn grasses.

If the grass gets overgrown before you can mow it, don't be tempted to just whack it down to its normal height; this drastic pruning is a fast and easy way to weaken the grass and make it more problem-prone later on. Instead, raise the height of your mower blade so you only cut off the top inch (2.5 cm) of grass. Wait a day or two, then cut off another inch (2.5 cm). Continue

Lay out garden beds with smooth curves or straight lines. Avoid sharp angles, which make mowing more of a chore.

this process until the grass is back at its ideal height. Sure, it's a little more work. But the few extra hours you take for proper mowing now will be amply rewarded by the continuing health of your turf.

Watering

Shocking as this might seem, some respected and knowledgeable professionals in horticulture do not water their lawns. They know that grasses go dormant during hot weather to save energy and conserve water. The lawn will stop growing (reducing mowing chores) and may turn off-color, but the cooler temperatures and more abundant moisture of fall will bring a dramatic recovery.

You may be uncomfortable with this approach. And equally respected and knowledgeable professionals in horticulture argue that a vigorous, watered lawn competes better with weeds and better resists pests. But if you really want a low-maintenance yard, you may decide to skip the watering routine altogether and know you're in good company.

If you do decide to water, water when your grass shows that it needs it rather than by a set schedule. It's time to water when the grass looks duller than usual and doesn't bounce back right away when you step on it. Your grass will be healthier if you water deeply and slowly, rather than

If you irrigate your lawn, water slowly and deeply.

Make Mowing Easier

Reduce your mowing time by making the job simpler. Here are some tried-and-true tips for easy lawn mowing:

- Remove the sod at the base of hard-to-trim-around trees, and add a layer of mulch or a planting of groundcovers instead.
- Install edgings and mowing strips around flower beds and tree and shrub plantings to make mowing simpler. (This also eliminates tedious trimming and weeding to keep grass out of beds.)
- Avoid using sharp angles and curves when you lay out garden beds; it's easier to mow along straight lines and smooth curves.
- Leave clippings on the lawn, unless they form piles that could smother the grass.

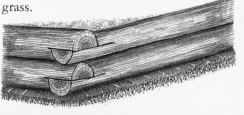

Don't mow your grass according to a set schedule. Let it grow to its ideal height and you'll likely mow less often.

frequently. Irrigate until the water penetrates the soil to about 6 inches (15 cm). That translates to about 1 inch (2.5 cm) of water at a time. To prevent runoff, water at 30- to 60-minute intervals (on for that long, then off for the same amount of time) rather than constantly. Or leave the water on, but rotate the sprinkler around the yard, repeating the circuit two or three times. Better yet, invest in an irrigation system that will deliver a slow, steady water supply right where it's needed.

Fertilizing

Maybe you've never fertilized your lawn. After all, why would you want to encourage the grass to grow *more?* Well, fertilizing correctly—at the right time and with the right organic materials—will help produce a healthier, thicker lawn, with deep roots that resist drought and top growth that chokes out weeds and shrugs off pest and disease problems. And unlike quickly dissolved chemical fertilizers, organic materials release their nutrients slowly over the season, so you won't see spurts of fast grass growth that follow traditional fertilizer applications.

Adjust mower blades to keep your lawn at its ideal height.

Apply mulch around shrubs to reduce mowing and trimming.

The easiest way to fertilize is to let the grass clippings fall on the lawn. As the clippings break down, they provide nutrients for future grass growth. However, if you've let the grass get so long that the mower leaves small haystacks in its wake, you should rake up the mats and add them to the compost pile.

To give your grass a real boost, though, a separate spring fertilizer application can't be beat. You'll encourage the grass to get an early start, so it will shade the soil and discourage weed seeds from sprouting. Spread a thin layer of an organic fertilizer such as compost or well-rotted manure evenly over the lawn. These materials will release their nutrients over a period of time, encouraging slow, steady growth. One application should be enough if you live in the North; in the South, with its long growing season, spring and fall applications are recommended.

Ideal Grass Heights

It's time to mow when your turf is one-quarter to one-third taller than the grass' ideal height. Look at the guidelines below to see what height your grass grows best at. (The lower number is for cool-weather or shady sites; raise the mower during warm weather.) Not sure what kinds of grass you have? Ask your local Cooperative Extension Service for help in identifying them.

Annual rye: 2 to 2½ inches (5 to 6.2 cm)
Bermudagrass: 1 to 1½ inches (2.5 to 3.7 cm)
Buffalograss: 3 to 4 inches (7.5 to 10 cm)
Fine fescue: 1½ to 2½ inches (3.7 to 6.2 cm)
Kentucky bluegrass: 2½ to 3 inches (6.2 to 7.5 cm)
St. Augustine grass: 2 to 3 inches (5 to 7.5 cm)
Tall fescue: 2½ to 3½ inches (6.2 to 8.7 cm)
Zoysiagrass: 1 to 1½ inches (2.5 to 3.7 cm)

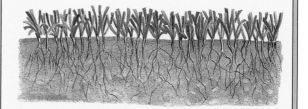

Cut down on mowing time by replacing some of your lawn with beautiful wildflowers or easy-care groundcovers.

Reducing Lawn Area

An obvious but surefire way to save yourself mowing time is by growing less grass. There are plenty of ways to cut down on mowing areas without plants. Build a deck or patio. Line the area below the swing set with landscape fabric and cover it with bark nuggets. Eliminate grass from hard-to-mow areas and replace it with an easy-to-maintain mulch.

A scythe can be a handy tool for cutting back your meadow in late winter.

All of these solutions have their place. But they don't cool things off as a big area covered with plants can, and they just aren't as soothing to the eye. If you like growing things but want to mow less, wildflowers or groundcovers may be the answer.

Wonderful Wildflowers

Wildflower meadows are fairly easy and inexpensive to grow from seed, and they provide a natural, easy-care solution for sunny spots. Meadow gardens will also attract a wide range of butterflies, birds, and beneficial insects to your yard.

Although they require less care than a lawn, wildflower meadows are *not* no maintenance. They will take some time to establish, and they do require some weeding, as well as yearly mowing. Also keep in mind that what you see as a meadow garden may simply be a patch of weeds to your neighbors. Discuss your plans with neighbors and check local mowing ordinances before you begin to avoid misunderstandings and complaints as you convert your lawn into a meadow.

Getting Started   To get the seeds off to a good start, you'll need to prepare the soil well, as you would for a new lawn. (See "Starting a New Lawn" on page 43 for details.) Getting rid of weeds before you plant is a key step. Let the prepared seedbed sit for several weeks so any exposed weed seeds can germinate; then hoe or till the site shallowly to kill the weeds. Repeat once or twice more before you plant. Or, in summer, cover the prepared, moistened seedbed with a sheet of clear plastic, and mound soil over the edges to seal the sheet. Leave it for 4 to 6 weeks; then remove the plastic and sow the seeds. This process, called solarization, will kill many surface weed seeds.

Plant wildflowers during your rainy season, evenly scattering a mixture of native wildflower seeds and native grasses on the soil surface and raking them in. It's worth the trouble to track down a mix of true natives; if you buy a "one-size-fits-all" mix, you'll pay for some seed that won't grow where you live. Ask your Cooperative Extension Service or local botanical garden to recommend plants that will grow well in your area.

Kill Weeds Before You Plant

Before planting wildflowers or groundcovers, you need a clean, weed-free site. Remove any perennial weeds, dig or till to loosen the soil, and rake the seedbed smooth. Then try one of the methods below.

Let exposed weed seeds germinate, then hoe or till shallowly.

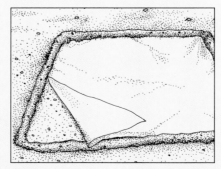
Cover the soil with clear plastic during summer to kill weed seeds.

Meadow Maintenance   If rains fail after you sow, water lightly and often to keep the soil moist while the seeds germinate. It takes about three seasons for a wildflower meadow to completely fill in, though you should have some pleasing results the first year. Pull out weedy plants until the meadow is full enough to shade them out. In late winter, use a sickle-bar mower, a scythe, or just a pair of hand clippers (if you have a small plot) to cut the now-brown meadow to about 6 inches (15 cm) high; this will keep woody plants from taking over and will scatter seeds for the new season.

Great Groundcovers

If wildflowers are a little too wild for you, groundcovers are another fine alternative to lawns. They are also great for reducing trimming chores along walls and fences and under tree and shrub plantings.

You can find a groundcover suited to just about any site and taste. Groundcovers can be creeping vines, low-growing perennials, or clumpy shrubs. Along with attractive deciduous or evergreen foliage, they may offer showy flowers and fruits. Some prefer shade, some like sun; others can take a bit of both. One thing most groundcovers can't take is foot traffic. Mulch or lawn is still the best choice for heavily trampled areas.

Choosing Good Groundcovers   There are so many terrific groundcovers to choose from that it's hard to know where to start. Begin by identifying the conditions where you want the plants to grow: Is the site sunny or shady? Is the soil moist or dry? Then think about how tall the groundcover can be; heights range from a few inches (centimeters) to a few feet (meters). If you're planting on a slope, you need a fast-spreading, dense groundcover to prevent erosion. You'll find growing information for some of the most popular groundcovers in "Low-maintenance Groundcovers" starting on page 48.

Getting Started   Just like lawns and meadows, groundcover plantings grow best in well-prepared soil. Remove any sod and weeds, and loosen the soil

---

Simple Planting on Steep Slopes

If you're turning a steep, grassy slope over to groundcovers, try this tip: Cover the area with black plastic for several weeks to fill the grass. Then remove the plastic, and plant your groundcovers right into the dead sod. The sod will keep the soil from washing away as the groundcovers get established. Top off the planting with a layer of mulch for good looks.

thoroughly, working in a ½- to 1-inch (1 to 2.5 cm) layer of compost or other organic matter. Rake the surface smooth, and you're ready to plant.

A general rule of thumb for spacing is to set plants 1 to 3 feet (30 to 90 cm) apart; use the closer spacing for small or slow-growing species, and the farther one for larger plants or fast growers. At these spacings, most groundcovers will take about 3 years to form a solid carpet. If you want faster results, use closer spacings, but keep in mind that the project will then cost more, since you'll need to buy more plants.

Caring for Groundcovers   Because some groundcovers can take a few years to completely cover the soil, mulch with straw, chopped leaves, or a similar light material to prevent erosion and suppress weeds. Or plant annuals in the bare spots. Water and weed regularly until plants are established (usually by the end of the first season). For extra interest, try interplanting with spring bulbs like crocus and daffodils. The groundcover will help to hide the ripening bulb foliage.

Groundcovers are an excellent alternative to grass in hard-to-mow areas, such as rocky sites; they also eliminate difficult mowing and tedious trimming around shrubs and trees.

Ajuga reptans   Labiatae

AJUGA

Ajuga is a fast-spreading groundcover for sun or shade. In spring, the leafy rosettes are topped with blue bloom spikes; add variety with pink- or white-flowered cultivars.

SEASON OF INTEREST: Showy spikes of deep blue flowers in late spring or early summer. The green, burgundy, or multicolored foliage is attractive during the growing season and in warm climates even into the winter.

BEST CLIMATE AND SITE: Zones 3–9. Full sun to light shade (more shade in warm climates); moist soil.

GROWING GUIDELINES: Add organic matter to the bed before planting. Water during drought. Weed out off-type seedlings—those that don't have the same leaf or flower color. Fertilize in early spring with compost or a complete organic fertilizer (one with similar percentages of nitrogen, phosphorus, and potassium).

PEST AND DISEASE PREVENTION: Avoid hot, dry locations, which encourage spider mites. To prevent root or crown rots, stay away from heavy shade and wet soil.

LANDSCAPE USE: Grows to 4–6 inches (10–15 cm). Plant 4–8 inches (10–20 cm) apart. Ajuga is an excellent groundcover, but it won't tolerate foot traffic. Plant near flowers such as *Muscari armeniacum,* white violets, or pink tulips to harmonize with flower or foliage colors.

OTHER COMMENTS: For variety in flower color, try white-flowered 'Alba' or pink-flowered 'Pink Beauty'.

Bergenia cordifolia   Saxifragaceae

HEART-LEAVED BERGENIA

The succulent green foliage of heart-leaved bergenia is attractive all year long. In cooler areas, the clumps may be topped with short flower clusters in spring or fall.

SEASON OF INTEREST: Mauve, red, pink, or white flowers in early spring and occasionally in fall. Through the rest of the growing season, you'll enjoy the lettuce-like heads of lustrous, leathery foliage that can reach 8 inches (20 cm) across.

BEST CLIMATE AND SITE: Zones 3–6; it will grow but may not flower as well in Zones 7–8. Full sun (partial shade in hotter locations); moist, fertile, humus-rich soil.

GROWING GUIDELINES: Trim by hand or mow down the foliage with a lawn mower if it browns during winter. New leaves emerge in spring. Divide to renew every 4–6 years.

PEST AND DISEASE PREVENTION: Trap slugs and snails in saucers of beer, sunken shallowly in the soil near the plants. Check traps and remove pests daily.

LANDSCAPE USE: Height and width to 18 inches (45 cm). Space plants 10–20 inches (25–50 cm) apart. For maximum impact, plant in large groups as a groundcover, as an edging in a flower garden, or in a sweep under trees and shrubs.

RELATED PLANTS:
LEATHER BERGENIA (*B. crassifolia*): Grows to 12 inches (30 cm) tall; light pink flowers.

Convallaria majalis   Liliaceae

LILY-OF-THE-VALLEY

Lily-of-the-valley will produce a thick, weed-suppressing groundcover in cool-climate gardens with partial shade and moist soil. It tolerates heavy shade but flowers less.

SEASON OF INTEREST: Fragrant white, bell-shaped flowers in spring. Poisonous, bright orange berries follow in summer. (Remove the temptingly edible-looking berries if you have young children.) Thick-growing, upright leaves create a weed-suppressing carpet through the rest of the growing season.

BEST CLIMATE AND SITE: Best in cooler climates, (Zones 3–5). Performs adequately as far south as Zone 7, but will not spread as quickly. For best results, plant in partial shade and moist soil.

GROWING GUIDELINES: Enrich the garden bed with organic matter before planting. Side-dress in the fall with compost or a complete organic fertilizer. Water during drought. To prevent lily-of-the-valley from becoming invasive, contain it within a root barrier, like metal or plastic edging.

PEST AND DISEASE PREVENTION: Avoid hot, dry sites to discourage spider mites and dieback.

LANDSCAPE USE: Height to 8 inches (20 cm). Space plants 4–8 inches (10–20 cm) apart. Plant lily-of-the-valley where it has room to spread freely. You also can cut the flowers. Try it in front of a shade garden, combined with broad-leaved hostas for contrast.

OTHER COMMENTS: Double-flowered 'Flore Pleno' may not spread as quickly as the species. 'Rosea' has light pink flowers.

| *Cotoneaster horizontalis* Rosaceae | *Euonymus fortunei* Celastraceae |

ROCKSPRAY COTONEASTER

WINTERCREEPER

Showy rockspray cotoneaster is an excellent choice for planting along walls and banks, where it can cascade gracefully. Enjoy the blooms in spring and berries in fall.

Evergreen wintercreeper can grow as a vine or as a low-spreading woody shrub, depending on the cultivar. Try the shrubby 'Emerald 'n Gold' to brighten a shady spot.

SEASON OF INTEREST: Small but abundant pink or white flowers in late May and early June. Glossy green foliage covers herringbone-patterned branches during the summer. Red berries in the fall.

BEST CLIMATE AND SITE: Zones 5–9. In Zone 7 and south, rockspray cotoneaster may be evergreen. For best results, plant in full sun or light shade and a fertile, well-drained soil. Will tolerate dry soil, sand, salt spray, wind, and medium shade.

GROWING GUIDELINES: Enrich the planting bed with organic matter and mulch if the soil is dry. Prune off dead wood anytime.

PEST AND DISEASE PREVENTION: To avoid diseases, buy disease-free nursery stock and give it the growing conditions it needs to stay vigorous. If fire blight strikes an existing plant, remove and destroy the blackened, curling stem, along with 6 inches (15 cm) of healthy growth. Inspect the plant occasionally for insect pests and treat them with insecticidal soap, light horticultural oil, or a botanical insecticide.

LANDSCAPE USE: Grows to 2–3 feet (60–90 cm) tall. Space plants 3–5 feet (90-150 cm) apart. Mass them in shrub beds and mixed borders or on banks.

RELATED PLANTS:

CRANBERRY COTONEASTER (*C. apiculatus*): Height to 3 feet (90 cm); width to 6 feet (1.8 m). Pink flowers; irregular branching.

SEASON OF INTEREST: Attractive, glossy green foliage all year long. The leaves of some cultivars are touched with gold, white, or pink. In the fall, pink fruits display red-coated seeds.

BEST CLIMATE AND SITE: Zones 5–9. Full sun to moderate shade; well-drained soil. Avoid sites that are hot and dry.

GROWING GUIDELINES: Grows easily and tolerates short periods of drought. Irrigate during extended dry weather for best results. Rejuvenate the foliage by pruning off the upper third of the stem every few years.

PEST AND DISEASE PREVENTION: To avoid problems, buy disease-free plants and keep them growing vigorously. If leaf spots or powdery mildew strike, destroy fallen leaves. Watch for scale, which is less troublesome on 'Green Lane'. Control aphids and thrips with insecticidal soap.

LANDSCAPE USE: Height about 6 inches (15 cm). Space plants 2–3 feet (60–90 cm) apart. Will cover the ground or climb up to 70 feet (21 m) on a tree or building. Use in small clumps in shrub or mixed flower gardens.

OTHER COMMENTS: The variety *coloratus* turns bronze in winter.

RELATED PLANTS: See the Burning bush (*E. alata*) entry on page 77.

Galium odoratum　　　　　　　　　　　Rubiaceae

SWEET WOODRUFF

If you have a moist, shady spot, don't struggle to grow grass there—try sweet woodruff instead. Woodruff has attractive green foliage and tiny white flowers in spring.

SEASON OF INTEREST: Covered with tiny, fragrant white flowers in spring. The whorled, green foliage is attractive through fall.

BEST CLIMATE AND SITE: Zones 4–8. Light to medium shade; moist soil.

GROWING GUIDELINES: Water when the soil dries out. Top-dress with compost before the shoots emerge in spring.

PEST AND DISEASE PREVENTION: To discourage dieback in hot and humid locations, plant sweet woodruff in medium shade. If a planting does wilt and disappear, it probably will resprout in cooler weather.

LANDSCAPE USE: Grows to 4–9 inches (10–22.5 cm) tall. Space plants 4–12 inches (10–30 cm) apart. Will spread readily but not invasively. Use in large sweeps in a mixed border, beneath shade trees, or in a woodland garden. Plant with white-flowered azaleas (*Rhododendron* spp.) or yellow and white daffodils.

RELATED PLANTS:

YELLOW BEDSTRAW (*G. verum*): Similar whorled leaves and yellow flowers during the summer.

Hedera helix　　　　　　　　　　　Araliaceae

ENGLISH IVY

English ivy is a great groundcover for shady sites. Some cultivars, like yellow 'Buttercup', have colorful leaves; other cultivars produce the usual glossy green foliage.

SEASON OF INTEREST: The lustrous evergreen foliage is attractive throughout the year. Choose cultivars with traditional dark green leaves or those that are marked with gold or white.

BEST CLIMATE AND SITE: Zones 5–9. Light shade; moist, rich, well-drained soil. Tolerates heavy shade. In Zone 5, plant extra-hardy cultivars like 'Thorndale' or 'Wilson's'.

GROWING GUIDELINES: For quick growth, prepare the planting bed with organic matter and keep it moist until the ivy begins to spread. Pull weeds that may move in, especially in sunny areas. Trim lanky vines with pruners or a string trimmer in early spring to encourage compact growth.

PEST AND DISEASE PREVENTION: Avoid diseases by growing ivy in a location with good air circulation. Thin plantings that get overcrowded. To avoid spreading diseases like leaf spot or powdery mildew, don't move through the ivy when the leaves are wet. Remove and destroy diseased plants. Avoid hot, dry conditions, which make ivy more susceptible to spider mites. Treat aphids, scale, and mealybugs with light horticultural oil.

LANDSCAPE USE: Height to 10 inches (25 cm). Space plants 6–24 inches (15–60 cm) apart. Use under trees and shrubs, in foundation plantings, or to combat erosion on shady banks. Combine with large clusters of daffodils.

CREEPING JUNIPER

Creeping juniper is a dependable shrubby groundcover for hot, dry sites. 'Wiltonii' (also sold as 'Blue Rug') is a particularly flat-growing cultivar with silver-blue foliage.

SEASON OF INTEREST: Handsome blue-green foliage turns plum purple in winter, providing year-round interest.

BEST CLIMATE AND SITE: Zones 3–9. Full sun. You can plant it in hot, dry conditions and soil that is heavy, rocky, or mildly alkaline but not soggy.

GROWING GUIDELINES: Older plants can become barren at the base, limiting their effectiveness as a groundcover. Prune stems back to a sideshoot that will grow toward an open, unfoliated section of the plant and fill it in.

PEST AND DISEASE PREVENTION: Minimize the risk of juniper blight by planting in low-humidity climates in full sun; choose a site with good air circulation. Cut off and destroy infected branches on a sunny day. You also should cut off the spiky balls formed by cedar-apple rust.

LANDSCAPE USE: Height to 2 feet (60 cm). Space plants 3–5 feet (90–150 cm) apart. Although it doesn't grow quickly, it will colonize difficult sites on slopes, around foundations, on rocky slopes or banks, and in containers. Keep it away from play areas or sites where the branches could be broken under foot or heavy snow.

RELATED PLANTS:

SHORE JUNIPER (*J. conferta*): Height to 3 feet (90 cm); width to 6 feet (1.8 m). Hardy to Zone 6; black cones.

SPOTTED LAMIUM

The delicate, silvery leaves of spotted lamium can really light up a shady spot. 'Beacon Silver' has purplish pink flowers; other cultivars have white or pink blooms.

SEASON OF INTEREST: Spikes of purplish pink flowers in late spring and early summer. The silver-and-green foliage looks good throughout the growing season.

BEST CLIMATE AND SITE: Zones 4–8. Light to medium shade; moist, well-drained soil. Too much sun can burn the leaves.

GROWING GUIDELINES: In warmer areas, you may need to trim lamium in midsummer to keep it from growing lanky. The species can become weedy; stick with cultivars. Water during drought.

PEST AND DISEASE PREVENTION: Spotted lamium can die back in hot, dry summer weather. Avoid it by planting 'White Nancy', which is less susceptible to dieback.

LANDSCAPE USE: Grows to 6 inches (15 cm) tall. Space plants 6–12 inches (15–30 cm) apart. Use as a groundcover or edging in a flower or shrub border. Or spread a large mass under a tree. For contrast, combine it with the large heart-shaped leaves of Siberian bugloss (*Brunnera macrophylla*), the arching fronds of white bleeding heart (*Dicentra spectabilis* 'Alba') or the upright flowers of black snakeroot (*Cimicifuga racemosa*).

OTHER COMMENTS: Cultivars like 'White Nancy' and 'Album' have white flowers. 'Pink Pewter' has soft pink flowers. 'Beedham's White' offers yellow foliage and white flowers.

Liriope spicata   Liliaceae

CREEPING LILYTURF

Creeping lilyturf forms a tough evergreen groundcover for sun or shade. Surround it with an edging to keep lawn grass from growing in and lilyturf from spreading out.

SEASON OF INTEREST: Spikes of pale purple or nearly white flowers in summer. Throughout the rest of the growing season and late into winter, you'll enjoy the attractive grass-like leaves.

BEST CLIMATE AND SITE: Zones 5–10. Full sun for the best flowering, but will tolerate light or medium shade; moist but well-drained soil.

GROWING GUIDELINES: Remove scraggly old flower stalks. Mow down the yellow leaves in early winter.

PEST AND DISEASE PREVENTION: Don't let grass creep into this planting: You may never be able to separate the two. Use an edging around the garden to keep grass out and creeping lilyturf in.

LANDSCAPE USE: Height to 12 inches (30 cm). Space plants 6–12 inches (15–30 cm) apart. Not as aggressive as other groundcovers, so you can safely plant it in smaller gardens or flower beds. Use lilyturf as an edging or groundcover under trees or shrubs. Combine with plants with bold foliage like coleus in light shade or variegated impatiens in sun.

RELATED PLANTS:
BIG BLUE LILYTURF (*L. muscari*): Height to 18 inches (45 cm); broader leaves than *L. spicata*. Hardy to Zone 7; thick spikes of violet flowers.

Ophiopogon japonicus   Liliaceae

DWARF MONDO GRASS

A planting of dwarf mondo grass produces tidy, low mats of dark green, grass-like foliage. It is a great replacement for lawn in shady spots under trees and shrubs.

SEASON OF INTEREST: Neat, grass-like, dark green leaves. In summer it produces white or purple flowers that mature to blue berries, but they seldom peer above the leaves.

BEST CLIMATE AND SITE: Zones 6–9. Light shade; well-drained, fertile soil.

GROWING GUIDELINES: Not an aggressive spreader. Weed around it for a year or two after planting until it becomes dense enough to discourage weeds.

PEST AND DISEASE PREVENTION: Plants are generally problem-free.

LANDSCAPE USE: Grows to 6–15 inches (15–37.5 cm) tall. Use in sweeps around trees and shrubs. Or set smaller clumps in flower gardens to separate conflicting bloom colors.

RELATED PLANTS:
BLACK MONDO GRASS (*O. planiscapus* var. *nigrescens*): Deep purple leaves and white or slightly pinkish flowers. Makes a showy contrast to plants with light green- or yellow-variegated foliage, like hostas or ferns.

JAPANESE PACHYSANDRA

Japanese pachysandra is a popular choice for covering the ground along paths and walls and under trees and shrubs. Combine it with tall spring bulbs for extra interest.

SEASON OF INTEREST: Whorled clusters of medium green leaves year-round. Some cultivars are variegated.

BEST CLIMATE AND SITE: Zones 4–7. Light to heavy shade; rich, well-drained soil. Too much sun or wind makes the foliage yellow.

GROWING GUIDELINES: Enrich planting beds with organic matter. Top-dress mature plantings with 1 inch (2.5 cm) of compost every year or two. If growth becomes lanky, cut the shoots back about 3 inches (7.5 cm) in spring.

PEST AND DISEASE PREVENTION: Water during drought to prevent dieback and spider mite attack. To avoid leaf blight, thin overcrowded growth; to remedy it, remove and destroy unhealthy stems.

LANDSCAPE USE: Height to 12 inches (30 cm). Space plants 8–12 inches (20–30 cm) apart. Spreads quickly beneath trees or shrubs or in the dense shade beside walls. Will often grow where other plants have failed. But keep it away from paths; it'll be crushed if stepped on. Combine Japanese pachysandra with sturdy stemmed bulbs like daffodils that can push up through the foliage.

RELATED PLANTS:

ALLEGHENY PACHYSANDRA (*P. procumbens*): This deciduous groundcover will carpet the ground with short spikes of small white flowers in early spring before the leaves emerge.

CREEPING PHLOX

Add a touch of color to moist, shady sites with spring-blooming creeping phlox. This beautiful evergreen groundcover forms broad, dense clumps of spreading stems.

SEASON OF INTEREST: Lavish display of ¾-inch (18 mm) wide blue, pink, or white flowers in spring.

BEST CLIMATE AND SITE: Zones 2–8. Light to medium shade; moist, rich soil.

GROWING GUIDELINES: Deadhead with hedge shears or grass clippers. Top-dress with 1 inch (2.5 cm) of compost in spring before the new shoots emerge. Water during drought.

PEST AND DISEASE PREVENTION: Plants are generally problem-free.

LANDSCAPE USE: Height to 12 inches (30 cm). Space plants 8–12 inches (20–30 cm) apart. Grows slowly but densely. Use in large masses beneath shade trees. Combine 'Bruce's White' with spring-blooming viburnums (*Viburnum* spp.) and white tulips.

RELATED PLANTS:

Phlox x *procumbens:* Combines the vigor of moss pink (*P. subulata*) with the larger flowers of creeping phlox. The variety *variegata* has deciduous white-variegated leaves that remain interesting after the purplish pink flowers have faded.

Phlox subulata   Polemoniaceae

MOSS PINK

Moss pink forms mats of needle-like evergreen leaves topped with colorful flowers in early spring. After bloom, trim plants with shears to promote compact growth.

SEASON OF INTEREST: This evergreen erupts with blue, white, or purple flowers in early spring. The mat-forming foliage, which looks like moss, remains attractive for the rest of year.

BEST CLIMATE AND SITE: Zones 2–9. Full sun; well-drained soil. Tolerates light shade, especially in hot locations.

GROWING GUIDELINES: Pull out grasses and perennial weeds. After bloom, trim with hedge shears or grass clippers to remove spent blooms and promote compact growth.

PEST AND DISEASE PREVENTION: Plants are generally problem-free.

LANDSCAPE USE: Grows to 6–9 inches (15–22.5 cm) tall. Space plants 12–16 inches (30–60 cm) apart. Let it creep across the front of a flower garden or along banks and through rock gardens.

RELATED PLANTS: See the Creeping phlox (*P. stolonifera*) entry.

Potentilla tridentata   Rosaceae

THREE-TOOTHED CINQUEFOIL

Three-toothed cinquefoil is an excellent groundcover for rocky sites and dry, sunny slopes. The leaves often turn reddish in fall; they may be evergreen in warm climates.

SEASON OF INTEREST: Small, white, strawberry-like flowers appear in early summer. The deep green, fan-shaped or three-part leaves remain attractive through the growing season. During fall in cool climates they turn handsome dark red and then drop. Can stay evergreen in warmer climates.

BEST CLIMATE AND SITE: Zones 2–7. Full sun; dry, acid soil.

GROWING GUIDELINES: Water in drought.

PEST AND DISEASE PREVENTION: Plants are generally problem-free.

LANDSCAPE USE: Grows to 6–12 inches (15–30 cm) tall. Space plants 8–12 inches (20–30 cm) apart. Use this creeper in rock gardens or on dry banks. It will spread despite arid conditions.

RELATED PLANTS: There are many other *Potentilla* species that do well in sun and well-drained soils. See the shrubby cinquefoil (*P. fruticosa*) entry on page 85.

Sedum kamtschaticum   Crassulaceae

KAMSCHATKA SEDUM

Cover dry, rocky areas with the sprawling stems and succulent toothed leaves of Kamschatka sedum. The foliage of the cultivar 'Variegatum' has an attractive creamy edging.

SEASON OF INTEREST: A sprinkling of starry yellow flowers appear over succulent toothed leaves through summer. You also can find flashy, variegated forms.

BEST CLIMATE AND SITE: Zones 3–8. Full sun; light shade south of Zone 6; well-drained, fertile soil. Drought-tolerant.

GROWING GUIDELINES: Fertilize in early spring with compost or a complete organic fertilizer (one with similar percentages of nitrogen, phosphorus, and potassium). Deadhead occasionally. Cut back the old stems in fall.

PEST AND DISEASE PREVENTION: Prevent diseases by planting in well-drained soil and thinning overcrowded growth.

LANDSCAPE USE: Height to 9 inches (22.5 cm). Space plants 6–12 inches (15–30 cm) apart. Kamschatka sedum has an open habit that may not be dense enough to crowd out weeds, but it is attractive on banks and in rocky soils where other plants grow poorly. It makes a nice companion for gold-variegated Adam's-needle (*Yucca filamentosa*).

RELATED PLANTS:

GOLDENMOSS SEDUM (*S. acre*): Height to 3 inches (7.5 cm); bears prolific displays of yellow flowers in spring and summer. Can be invasive in moist soil.

Thymus serpyllum   Labiatae

MOTHER-OF-THYME

Mother-of-thyme is an easy-to-grow, fast-spreading groundcover for sunny, well-drained sites. Clusters of tiny flowers top the aromatic evergreen leaves in late spring.

SEASON OF INTEREST: Bears pink, red, or white flowers in late spring. This petite, aromatic evergreen may bloom again in summer. Cultivars have variegated, yellow, or wooly leaves that can be as interesting as the flowers.

BEST CLIMATE AND SITE: Zones 4–7. Full sun; well-drained, slightly alkaline, sandy soil.

GROWING GUIDELINES: Fertilize or mulch with organic matter sparingly, if at all, or the plant will get spindly and floppy. Pull weeds as they appear.

PEST AND DISEASE PREVENTION: Prevent root rot with well-drained soil.

LANDSCAPE USE: Height to 1 inch (2.5 cm). Space plants 8–12 inches (20–30 cm) apart. Set loose on dry slopes or stone walls. Spread between stones in a walk or patio.

Tiarella cordifolia   Saxifragaceae

ALLEGHENY FOAMFLOWER

Allegheny foamflower is a delightful alternative to grass in a shady spot. Its spikes of white or pink flowers bloom in spring over spreading clumps or heart-shaped leaves.

SEASON OF INTEREST: Sends spikes of small, white or pink flowers over rosettes of lobed leaves in spring. The leaves may turn purplish in winter.

BEST CLIMATE AND SITE: Zones 3–8. Medium to heavy shade; rich, moist soil.

GROWING GUIDELINES: Enrich the planting bed with organic matter before planting and mulch occasionally with 1 inch (2.5 cm) of compost. Deadhead after bloom.

PEST AND DISEASE PREVENTION: Plants are generally problem-free.

LANDSCAPE USE: Grows to 6–12 inches (15–30 cm) tall. Space plants 12–18 inches (30–45 cm) apart. Plant in large clumps in a woodland garden, in sweeps in a shaded wildflower border, or in large patches beneath shade trees. Combine foamflowers with other residents of moist deciduous woodlands like ferns and creeping phlox (*Phlox stolonifera*).

RELATED PLANTS:

WHERRY'S FOAMFLOWER (*T. wherryi*): Clusters of smaller pink or white flowers; doesn't spread like Allegheny foamflower.

Vinca minor   Apocynaceae

COMMON PERIWINKLE

Fast-growing common periwinkle is a popular groundcover for large shady areas. For extra interest, combine it with small bulbs to complement the glossy evergreen foliage.

SEASON OF INTEREST: The species explodes with blue flowers in spring; some cultivars flower in purple, pink, or light blue. The handsome, shiny, dark evergreen leaves make a good show through the rest of the year.

BEST CLIMATE AND SITE: Zones 4–9. All degrees of shade; rich, moist soil.

GROWING GUIDELINES: Tolerates drought once established, but you'll need to water young plants during dry spells. Pull out grass and other weeds that invade.

PEST AND DISEASE PREVENTION: Shelter from full sun during winter to prevent leaf yellowing.

LANDSCAPE USE: Height to 6 inches (15 cm). Space plants 6–12 inches (15–30 cm) apart. Use beneath trees and shrubs, on banks, and in rocky places. Or use as a vining accent in containers.

RELATED PLANTS:

BIG PERIWINKLE (*V. major*): Zones 7–9; has larger evergreen leaves, which are variegated or blotched with white in some cultivars.

Timesaving Trees
and Shrubs

Few things can make a house seem like part of its surroundings as trees and shrubs can. They shelter your house from the wind, attract birds and other wildlife, and give kids a place to climb. If they flower, they add color and fragrance to the landscape. Trees are especially good at creating shade, which both pleases the eye and (if the trees are properly placed) lowers your air-conditioning bill. Shrub plantings can give your yard privacy, block unattractive views, and define areas in what was once a shapeless expanse of yard. And best of all, these plants can be among the most low-maintenance elements in your yard.

Because trees and shrubs are such a valuable and permanent element of the landscape, it's especially important to choose them carefully, paying attention to their ultimate size, as well as any particular needs

they may have. Once you select the plants, you can prepare them for a long, healthy life by planting them properly and tending them well while they're young.

Once they're established, trees and shrubs are the epitome of low-maintenance plants for your landscape. You don't have to mow them, harvest them, or pinch off their dead flowers. And most of the care they might require, such as pruning or raking, can wait until fall or winter, when the rest of the landscape is making few demands on your time.

In this chapter, you'll learn how to choose trees and shrubs that you can live with. You'll find out how to plant them properly, so they'll grow well in the future, and how to care for them throughout the seasons. With just a little attention, well-chosen trees and shrubs can reward you with years of easy-care beauty.

Opposite: Think carefully when buying and siting new trees and shrubs. If you want to grow a plant with a messy habit—like the spiny seedpods of sweetgum (*Liquidambar styraciflua*)—site it in an out-of-the-way spot.

Choosing and Using Trees and Shrubs

It's a warm day in early spring, and you find yourself at your local garden center. As you stroll around the nursery yard, you see a tree you absolutely must have. What do you do?

If you really want a low-maintenance landscape, the answer is: *nothing.* Any time you add a new tree or shrub to your yard, always do some research before you buy. Find out how big the plant will get and how fast it grows. It may look small now, but it could take over half your yard in a few years without frequent pruning. Also make sure the plant is adapted to your climate and growing conditions. Below you'll find helpful details on picking the right plants for your low-maintenance landscape. To learn about specific trees and shrubs, see "Low-maintenance Trees and Shrubs," starting on page 68.

Size Up Your Selection

As you evaluate a tree or shrub, make sure its mature size is right for its purpose and the place you plan to put it. People make the same mistake with woody plants that they do with puppies: they underestimate how big they'll be when they grow up. Don't be deceived by how small trees and shrubs look in their containers. Before you buy one, do a little research on

Give your trees and shrubs enough room to develop to their full size—you'll minimize pruning later on.

how high and wide it will be at maturity. Check a few garden books, ask a few nurseries, and visit a few gardens. You'll find that individual plants, like individual people, vary in size. The soil and climate play a part in determining a plant's mature size, as does its genetic makeup. Your research will give you a feel for the range of heights and widths a plant might reach.

If the species you're considering might get too big for the spot you want to plant it, look for a similar but shorter-growing species or cultivar. If a plant wants to be big, don't figure that pruning will keep it small. The purpose of pruning is to remove damaged wood and improve a plant's shape, not to compensate for errors in judgment. And besides, you have better things to do with your time than to prune.

Avoid Plants with Annoying Habits

Along with mature size, take into account how much you'll have to clean up after the plant. Some trees drop twigs after every gusty storm. Others have messy fruit, like the spiky round seedpods of sweet gum (*Liquidambar styraciflua*) or the foul-smelling fleshy seeds of female ginkgo trees (*Ginkgo biloba*).

If you have your heart set on a tree with any of these antisocial characteristics, you can minimize the headache it causes by planting it away from walkways and your house. Rather than spending hours sweeping maple seeds from your patio, for instance, let them

River birch (*Betula nigra*) is a handsome tree that is much less problem-prone than many other birches.

Grouping trees and shrubs with perennials and groundcovers eliminates trimming around individual plants.

fall nearly unnoticed in the center of the yard. Or look for seedless cultivars of landscape plants, like 'Marshall's Seedless' ash (*Fraxinus pennsylvanica* 'Marshall's Seedless').

Investigate Potential Pest Problems

Consider how attractive the tree or shrub may be to pests. In general, vigorous plants attract fewer pests and withstand those that do find them. But if you can choose species and cultivars that are naturally more problem-resistant, you're several steps ahead of the game. A plant's susceptibility to insects and diseases can vary depending on where you live, so check with your Cooperative Extension Service or a nearby botanical garden to learn which pests are common in your area.

Consider Your Climate

A big part of a plant's vigor depends on how well adapted it is to your region and the site. For example, the white-barked canoe birch (*Betula papyrifera*) grows beautifully in Wisconsin, but it's an easy mark for birch borers in warmer Illinois. If you love a plant not suited to your yard or region, you can often get a similar look with another plant. River birch (*B. nigra*), for instance, has attractive bark and a similar growth habit to canoe birch, and river birch is less prone to birch borers.

A final word about pests: Planting a tree or shrub that's prone to a particular problem need not doom you to more work. Many insects and diseases look bad but don't really threaten the life of the plant. Lilacs, for example, often get powdery mildew, which is basically harmless and sometimes barely noticeable. If you *really* want the plant and are willing to put up with the pest or disease damage, the most low-maintenance solution to problems can be to just ignore them.

Troublesome Trees

While no tree is perfect, some species tend to be much more of a bother than others. These troublemakers may be weak-wooded (drop lots of branches that you have to pick up), produce massive quantities of annoying fruits or seeds or just have a combination of unattractive features. Below is a list of some common nuisance trees, along with their bad habits:

Acer platanoides (Norway maple): shallow-rooted, reseeds prolifically

Ailanthus altissima (tree-of-heaven): reseeds prolifically, odiferous male flowers

Albizia julibrissin (mimosa): pest- and disease-prone, messy seedpods

Morus spp. (mulberries): messy fruit, pest- and disease-prone

Populus spp. (poplars): weak-wooded, invasive roots, pest- and disease-prone

Salix spp. (willows): pest- and disease-prone, weak-wooded

Ulmus pumila (Siberian elm): weak-wooded, pest-prone

Foundation plantings don't have to be boring! Try a lively mixture of shrubs, trees, flowers, and groundcovers.

Easy-care Foundation Plantings

That small strip of soil that surrounds the bottom of the house may be the most misunderstood area in the landscape. All too often it's relegated to a boring hodgepodge of badly pruned evergreens, but it doesn't have to be that way. The two secrets to an interesting, attractive, and low-maintenance foundation planting are a simple design and well-chosen plants.

Designing a Foundation Planting

You could create a low-maintenance foundation planting by sticking in a straight row of dwarf evergreens and surrounding them with a layer of mulch. But with a little extra effort, you can combine a variety of plants for an interesting, dynamic planting scheme that is a pleasure to stroll by on your way in and out the door.

To make this work, you'll need to start with a design, so you can "see" how the plants will fit together before you buy and install them. At some point, your design should be on paper, drawn to scale. You may want to draw the plan first, then try to visualize how it will look in real life. Or you may find it easier to experiment with different layouts right on the site, and then record your best effort.

To help visualize the design, lay a rope along the ground to define a possible outline for the planting. Stick in upside-down brooms or tall stakes to represent small trees; inverted bushel baskets or buckets could stand for shrubs. As you decide where things should go, keep in mind that you'll be planting them out at least 1 foot (30 cm) beyond the drip line to protect them from rain falling off the roof. (Cover the unplanted area along the drip line with a layer of gravel or a row of flat rocks or pavement blocks to prevent erosion.) When you are pleased with the broom-and-basket layout, translate that design to paper.

A yearly application of organic mulch around foundation plantings can keep weeds down and improve the soil.

Shrubs with colorful foliage, like this barberry, make showy additions to a foundation planting even when not in bloom.

Picking the Right Plants

Once you have a pleasing design, you can select plants to fit it. The most important step to making your planting low maintenance is choosing plants that won't get too big or too wide. That may mean selecting dwarf shrub species or cultivars that won't grow up to block your windows. It may also mean planting far enough from the house for the plants to spread out. The second most important thing is choosing plants that are well adapted to the site conditions: the soil (especially its drainage) and the amount of light (including the light and heat that bounce off the house wall behind the planting).

For year-round interest, combine multiseason plants like kerria, dwarf rhododendron, and bergenia.

Foundation plantings have traditionally contained mostly evergreen conifers, such as yew and juniper, or broad-leaved evergreens, like azaleas and boxwood. Evergreens do add color and hide the foundation all year, but deciduous shrubs have their place, too. Many species—including dwarf fothergilla (*Fothergilla gardenii*) and Japanese kerria (*Kerria japonica*)—offer multiseason interest with flowers, fall color, or attractive stems. Also look for dwarf or slow-growing cultivars that will stay low without regular pruning. A few interesting choices include maroon 'Crimson Pygmy' barberry (*Berberis thunbergii* 'Crimson Pygmy'), white-flowered dwarf slender deutzia (*Deutzia gracilis* 'Nikko'), and dwarf cranberry bush virnum (*Viburnum opulus* 'Nanum').

Though there are many wonderful plants to choose from, limit your design to a few different species—not only will it look better, but you'll have fewer types of plants to care for. If you choose interesting species, you don't have to worry that the lack of diversity will be monotonous. Look for plants with attractive textures or growth habits or with interesting fruit, flowers, or bark. And don't forget groundcovers, which unify the planting and help link it with the house and the lawn beyond. Some also offer seasonal flowers, fruits, or fall color. (For specific ideas, see "Low-maintenance Groundcovers," starting on page 48.)

Proper Planting for Future Health

If you skimp on soil preparation for your annuals or vegetables one year, you'll know by their poor performance that you should do better next time. Stuff your new shade tree into a cramped, poorly prepared planting hole and there's not much you can do to make up for the mistake later on. You've spent the time and money to buy the best low-maintenance tree or shrub for your site. Now protect your investment by providing the best possible growing conditions so your plant can thrive with little extra help from you.

Survey the Site

Before you dig, take a few moments to make sure the planting spot is just right for the tree or shrub. Is the site far enough away from the house, the sidewalk, the driveway, and other plants to give the tree or shrub enough room to reach its potential mature size? Is the plant adapted to the soil drainage? If the plant is prone to diseases, does the area have good air circulation? If the site isn't perfect, fix it or find a better one.

Dig In

Follow the steps below to create the best possible growing conditions for your tree or shrub.

1. Dig a hole at least twice as wide as the existing root mass and as deep as the root mass. Angle the sides of the hole so they are widest at the top. Remove rocks and debris from the hole.

Make sure each tree and shrub has enough room to develop without crowding—you'll minimize diseases and pruning.

Good soil preparation will help get your carefully chosen plants off to a vigorous start for healthy future growth.

Don't Doctor the Dirt

For a long time, everyone recommended that you mix the soil you dug from the planting hole with organic matter such as compost or peat before filling in around the plant. Research shows, however, that roots often find the amended soil so pleasant that they stay in the hole instead of spreading into the less agreeable soil beyond it. The cramped roots quickly deplete available nutrients and moisture. And since the plant isn't well anchored, it's susceptible to being toppled by high winds. So hold off on the amendments, and your plants will be more likely to spread their roots and search out the nutrients and water they need to thrive.

One exception is balled-and-burlapped nursery plants, which are often grown in loose sandy soil and which can suffer if you plant them into an unamended heavy clay. If you have clayey soil and the soil in the root ball is on the sandy side, dig a wide planting hole and amend your soil with organic matter to loosen it and provide better drainage.

Planting

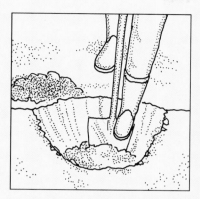

Dig a wide but shallow planting hole so new roots can spread easily.

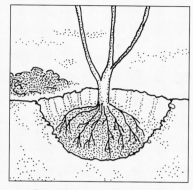

Spread the roots of bareroot plants evenly over a cone of soil.

Knock container plants out of the pot; set in the center of the hole.

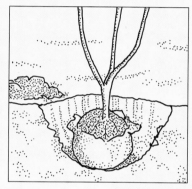

Set balled-and-burlapped plants in the hole; peel back the burlap.

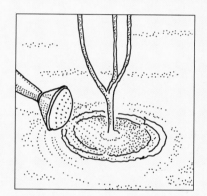

Water newly planted trees and shrubs well to encourage growth.

Depending on where you live, the best time to plant bareroot and balled-and-burlapped plants is fall, spring, or even late winter. Cool air temperatures will limit top growth, so the roots have a chance to grow and spread enough to support later growth. Fall and spring are also ideal for container plants, although they'll adapt to planting at just about anytime.

2. If your plant is bareroot (not balled-and-burlapped or in a container), make a mound of soil in the center to support it. Make sure the crown (the point where the trunk meets the roots) is even with the soil surface. Spread the roots as evenly as possible over the mound.

3. If your plant is in a pot, invert the container and gently slide the plant out without pulling on the stem. If you can't get the plant out, try tapping the bottom of the pot on the ground before inverting it. If that doesn't work, you may need to slice the pot open. Once you get the plant out, use a knife to make four lengthwise 1-inch (2.5 cm) cuts evenly spaced around the root ball. Then set the plant in the center of the hole.

4. If your plant is balled-and-burlapped, set it in the center of the hole. Cut the ropes or the top of the wire basket surrounding the root ball. If the wrapping material is natural burlap, just peel it back from the top of the root ball; the rest will rot away. If the wrapping material is synthetic or treated burlap, remove as much as you can without disturbing the roots, or at least slice the material open so the roots can grow out into the surrounding soil.

5. Add a stake if the tree leans to one side, is big enough to be top-heavy, or is little enough to get whipped around in the wind. Drive the stake firmly into the soil outside the root area.

6. Make sure the plant is straight, then fill in around the root ball or roots with the soil that you removed from the hole. Pat it down after every few inches (5 cm) to remove air pockets. The top of the root ball should be even with the soil surface.

7. Build a ridge around the outside of the planting hole to hold water. Fill the basin with water two or three times, letting it drain completely before refilling.

8. If you used a stake, attach the plant to the stake with strips of cotton fabric or other soft ties (to avoid damaging the bark). Leave some slack in the tie, so the tree can move a little in the wind; this movement will encourage stronger wood to develop. Remove the tie after 1 year.

While these directions apply for a single planting hole, remember that a key aspect of low maintenance is grouping plants together into large planting areas whenever possible. This eliminates having to mow and trim around individual plants and provides better growing conditions.

If rainfall is lacking, water new plantings regularly for the first 2 years, until plants are established.

Caring for Trees and Shrubs

One of the greatest things about trees and shrubs is that they don't need much day-to-day, or even week-to-week, maintenance. You need to do a few simple things to care for them while they're young and fewer simple things once they mature.

Special Care for New Plants

Water your new plants regularly (about once a week if you don't get any rain) for the first 2 years, until they can form enough roots to search out water on their own. To encourage a good root system, water deeply, slowly, and in an area wider than the end of the branches farthest from the trunk.

To make it easier to mow under trees and shrubs and to protect them from lawn-mower damage, leave a big grassless zone at the base. If you don't plant flowers or groundcovers under the trees, you can prevent weeds by putting down a weed barrier (like landscape fabric) or a 2- to 3-inch (5 to 7.5 cm) layer of mulch over the area. (Leave a mulch-free zone several inches wide around the trunk to discourage rot.)

Mulching around plants will help keep the soil moist and encourage root growth.

Maintaining Established Plants

Once your trees and shrubs are in and growing, they'll mostly take care of themselves. Unless you have a prolonged drought, established plantings should be able to scavenge the water they need from deep in the soil. Topping off organic mulches as they break down helps keep the soil evenly moist and discourages weeds.

Fertilizing   Trees and shrubs don't really need regular fertilizer applications since they can send roots long distances in search of needed nutrients. But for really good growth, spread a 1-inch (2.5 cm) layer of compost around each plant in spring. As it breaks down, the compost will slowly release a balanced dose of plant nutrients; it will also add organic matter to keep soil conditions ideal for good root growth. If you've used an

Think Twice about Plastic Mulch

Black plastic and landscape fabric (a sheet of porous plastic material) can both be effective and long-lasting weed barriers—especially when covered by an ornamental mulch such as washed river rock or bark nuggets. But before you use them around trees and shrubs, be aware that they do have some drawbacks.

Unlike organic mulches, plastic-based materials don't add any nutrients or organic matter to the soil, so you may need to apply extra nutrients for good plant growth. Solid plastic doesn't let air or water into the soil, so roots can suffocate or die from drought without extra-special attention (definitely not an aspect of low maintenance!). Landscape fabrics do let air and water in, but plant roots may grow up into them, creating real headaches if you ever want to remove the fabrics (they will need replacing every 5 to 7 years). And weeds that germinate on top of the fabric can root down into it, making them harder to pull.

What does this mean to you? Save the solid plastic mulches for the vegetable garden. If you need an easy-to-apply, trouble-free mulch to protect an area for a few years, landscape fabrics can be very handy. But for the best soil and plant health, and for real long-term, easy maintenance, groundcovers and organic mulches are the way to go.

Shrubs That Take Severe Pruning

If you have shrubs that are overgrown, you may be able to reclaim them with severe pruning. You can cut these shrubs down to about a foot (30 cm) above the ground and they'll grow back. Flowering shrubs may take a year or two off blooming after drastic pruning. For a more gradual approach, cut back one-third of the oldest stems each year over 3 years. Following is a list of some commonly grown shrubs that can tolerate severe pruning.

Abelia spp. (abelias); *Berberis* spp. (barberries); *Buddleia* spp. (butterfly bushes); *Buxus* spp. (boxwoods); *Callicarpa* spp. (beauty berries); *Deutzia* spp. (deutzias); *Forsythia* spp. (forsythias); *Hibiscus syriacus* (rose-of-Sharon); *Ligustrum* spp. (privets); *Lonicera* spp. (honeysuckles); *Myrica* spp. (bayberries); *Philadelphus* spp. (mock oranges); *Prunus laurocerasus* (cherry-laurel); *Rhus* spp. (sumacs); *Syringa* spp. (lilacs).

organic mulch, pull it back from the base of the plant, apply the compost, and replace the mulch. If you've used a landscape fabric, you'll have to remove it to put down the compost. Don't fertilize after midsummer in the North or early fall in the South; otherwise, the plants may produce succulent new growth that will be damaged by early fall frosts.

Pruning Pruning is perhaps the least understood and most poorly done aspect of tree and shrub maintenance. Why? Because people use it to reduce the size of plants they shouldn't have planted where they did in the first place. In truth, the real purpose of pruning is to remove wood that's damaged, dead, or growing in the wrong place or direction.

To prune shrubs and small trees correctly, start by removing any dead, diseased, crossing, or injured branches. On the trees, remove any suckers growing from the roots or the bottom of the trunk. If you're dealing with overgrown shrubs, you may decide to cut them down completely and let them sprout new growth or to just remove a few of the oldest stems each year. "Shrubs That Take Severe Pruning" lists some common shrubs that respond well to this treatment. Although much fuss is made about when to prune flowering shrubs, it's not a concern when you prune selectively, because you're only removing a few branches.

For your own safety, and for the plants' ultimate health, it's smart to leave pruning on large trees to professionals. As with small trees and shrubs, the only reason to prune large trees is to remove dead or damaged wood. Don't let anyone talk you into having your tree topped (a technique that shears the whole crown of the tree back to large stubs). Besides ruining the natural form and beauty of the tree, topping creates large wounds and crowded masses of succulent twigs that are easy targets for disease organisms.

A yearly application of compost can give plants the nutrients they need to grow vigorously and bloom prolifically.

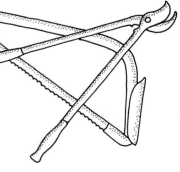

Prune thick stems with loppers or saws to make clean cuts.

Abelia x *grandiflora*   Caprifoliaceae

GLOSSY ABELIA

Glossy abelia is an easy-care shrub with multiseason interest —pink or white flowers from spring through summer and dark green leaves that turn purplish in winter.

SEASON OF INTEREST: White or pink bell-shaped flowers from May to August. The glossy, semigreen leaves may turn purple in winter.

BEST CLIMATE AND SITE: Zones 5–9, although the stems may die back to older wood or the roots during cold winters in the northern part of this range. Full sun and moist soil for the best flowers. Will also tolerate partial shade.

GROWING GUIDELINES: To encourage steady growth and prolong flowering, fertilize lightly in spring with a complete organic fertilizer—one with similar percentages of nitrogen, phosphorus, and potassium—or compost, and water during dry weather. Cut off long, old, unproductive branches anytime during the summer. In early spring, remove any dead wood.

PEST AND DISEASE PREVENTION: Plants are generally problem-free.

LANDSCAPE USE: Height 6–10 feet (1.8–3 m); width 4–6 feet (1.2–1.8 m). Slightly too large for most foundation plantings unless you choose compact cultivars. Try it in a shrub border, as a screen, or as a colorful backdrop for a flower garden.

OTHER COMMENTS: 'Prostrata' has white flowers. Height 2–3 feet (60–90 cm). 'Francis Mason'—hardy to Zone 6—has variegated foliage and pink flowers. Height 3–4 feet (90–120 cm).

Acer ginnala   Aceraceae

AMUR MAPLE

Adaptable amur maple is an excellent large shrub or small tree for a low-maintenance landscape. Its handsome dark green leaves often turn orange or red in early fall.

SEASON OF INTEREST: Bears fragrant strands of tiny flowers in April or May before the leaves emerge. The foliage turns yellow or red in early fall. Even after the leaves drop, you'll see winged seedpods, which can be bright red in cultivars like 'Red Fruit'.

BEST CLIMATE AND SITE: Zones 2–8. Full sun for the best fall color, although it will tolerate light shade. Tolerates various soil conditions, but grows best in moist, well-drained soil.

GROWING GUIDELINES: Before planting, remove turf from the rooting area; after planting, mulch to keep grass out. Fertilize with a complete organic fertilizer—one with similar percentages of nitrogen, phosphorus, and potassium—or compost every 2–3 years. Water during drought.

PEST AND DISEASE PREVENTION: Leaf spots can strike in warm climates. Clean up fallen leaves to prevent reinfection.

LANDSCAPE USE: Height 15–25 feet (4.5–7.5 m); similar spread. Use as the high point in a shrub border, to soften the corner of a large building, or to shade a patio.

RELATED PLANTS:

JAPANESE MAPLE (*A. palmatum*): Height 30 feet (9 m) or taller. Good-looking lobed or finely cut leaves and bright fall color.

Amelanchier arborea   Rosaceae

DOWNY SERVICEBERRY

Downy serviceberry forms an attractive large shrub or small tree. It bears white flowers in spring, followed by bird-attracting, edible, purple-black berries in summer.

SEASON OF INTEREST: Produces a brief bright show of white flower clusters in spring. In summer, edible purple-black fruits attract birds. During fall, the leaves turn red or orange.

BEST CLIMATE AND SITE: Zones 5–9. Tolerates light shade but produces better flowers and fall color in full sun. Plant in rich, moist, acid soil; will grow more slowly in average soil.

GROWING GUIDELINES: Water during drought to prevent early leaf drop.

PEST AND DISEASE PREVENTION: Prevent fire blight by fertilizing carefully: Avoid using high-nitrogen products, which produce soft, disease- susceptible growth. You also can spray the tree with bordeaux mixture in spring to prevent infection. If fire blight attacks, prune off the black, curling branches along with 4 inches (15 cm) of healthy growth.

LANDSCAPE USE: Height 15–30 feet (4.5–9 m). This subtle and beautiful native tree blends naturally into the edge of woodlands or the banks of brooks. Contrasts nicely with clusters of evergreens.

RELATED PLANTS:

APPLE SERVICEBERRY (*A.* x *grandiflora*): Pink-tinged buds and clusters of larger white flowers. Height to 25 feet (7.5 m).

Aucuba japonica   Cornaceae

JAPANESE AUCUBA

Accent a shady garden with the glossy evergreen leaves of Japanese aucuba. For a real show, choose a cultivar with yellow-speckled foliage, like 'Maculata'.

SEASON OF INTEREST: Enjoy the broad evergreen leaves all year. The foliage of some cultivars—including 'Crotonifolia' and 'Variegata'—is highlighted with yellow markings. If you have both male and female plants, you can also enjoy bright red berries in fall and winter.

BEST CLIMATE AND SITE: Zones 7–10. Grows best and produces the brightest leaves when protected from sun, wind, and heat. Tolerates dense shade and most well-drained soils.

GROWING GUIDELINES: Mulch sandy or dry soil with compost. Water when the soil begins to dry out. Remove individual long branches to shape; shearing will disfigure the foliage.

PEST AND DISEASE PREVENTION: Prevent pests by keeping the plant growing vigorously. Treat scale and mites with light horticultural oil; spray mealybug with insecticidal soap.

LANDSCAPE USE: Height 4–12 feet (1.2–3.6 m). Can be too tall for a foundation planting unless you prune regularly. Mass several plants in a shady shrub border for a bold sweep of color. Variegated foliage looks good with gold flowers like marigolds or zinnias. Combine a few with green plants that have contrasting texture, like lower-growing ferns.

Berberis thunbergii   Berberidaceae

JAPANESE BARBERRY

Japanese barberry comes in a variety of colors and sizes to fit almost any landscape. Many cultivars, such as 'Red Pillar', also offer phenomenal fall colors.

SEASON OF INTEREST: During the growing season, you'll enjoy Japanese barberry foliage: Different cultivars have green, yellow, or red-purple leaves. Small yellow flowers in late spring. In fall, the leaves turn red or orange; they drop to reveal small red fruits clinging to the branches.

BEST CLIMATE AND SITE: Zones 5–9. Full sun; dry to medium soil.

GROWING GUIDELINES: Prune out dead wood and shape in early spring.

PEST AND DISEASE PREVENTION: Plant in well-drained soil to avoid root rot.

LANDSCAPE USE: Height 3–6 feet (90–180 cm). Use small groups of this compact shrub in a foundation planting or mixed border. Or mass into a prickly hedge that will repel wild animals or frisky pets.

OTHER COMMENTS: The cultivar 'Aurea' has yellow leaves. Dwarf 'Crimson Pygmy' has red-purple leaves.

RELATED PLANTS:

KOREAN BARBERRY (*B. koreana*): Height 4–6 feet (1.2–1.8 m); produces larger leaves up to 3 inches (7.5 cm) long and 4-inch (10 cm) long drooping flower clusters.

MENTOR BARBERRY (*B.* x *mentorensis*): Matures at about 5 feet (1.5 m), is semi-evergreen, and makes a good screen or hedge.

Betula nigra   Betulaceae

RIVER BIRCH

If you have a site with moist, acid soil, try planting river birch. The peeling bark can reveal a variety of inner bark colors, from gray- to reddish brown.

SEASON OF INTEREST: Reddish brown, peeling bark is attractive year-round. During the growing season, river birch bears interesting, double-toothed leaves.

BEST CLIMATE AND SITE: Zones 4–8. Full sun; moist, fertile, acid soil; ideal near a stream or pond. Tolerates occasional flooding. Drier soil can make the tree smaller.

GROWING GUIDELINES: Water during drought.

PEST AND DISEASE PREVENTION: Plants are generally problem-free.

LANDSCAPE USE: Height 40–90 feet (12–27 m); width 40–60 feet (12–18 m). Use as a shade tree or waterside accent.

OTHER COMMENTS: The cultivar 'Heritage' has tan-colored bark. Height to 45 feet (13.5 m).

RELATED PLANTS:

HIMALAYAN BIRCH (*B. jacquemontii*): Height to 25 feet (7.5 m). This white-barked birch is resistant to bronze birch borer.

Buxus microphylla   Buxaceae

LITTLE-LEAVED BOXWOOD

Compact little-leaved boxwood is a handsome evergreen addition to foundation plantings. Also try it as a low hedge or as an edging to a flower or herb garden.

SEASON OF INTEREST: Small evergreen leaves are handsome through the growing season but can turn brownish in winter. In midspring, you may smell the hidden flowers' perfume.

BEST CLIMATE AND SITE: Zones 6–9. Full sun to medium shade; moist, well-drained soil. Avoid areas that are hot and dry, windy, or extra cold in winter.

GROWING GUIDELINES: Mulch with compost. Cut weeds growing in the shrub's rooting zone. Boxwood has shallow roots that are easy to damage with a hoe or hand weeder. If you use boxwood for a formal hedge or bed edging, shear as necessary.

PEST AND DISEASE PREVENTION: In poorly drained soil, plant in raised beds to eliminate root rot. Cover with pine boughs to prevent leaf scorch during the winter.

LANDSCAPE USE: Height and spread to 3–4 feet (90–120 cm). Compact forms can stay as low as 2 feet (60 cm) high. Use cultivars of the appropriate height to enclose flower borders or herb gardens. Group them into a small hedge or foundation planting.

RELATED PLANTS:

COMMON BOXWOOD (*B. sempervirens*): Height to 20 feet (6 m). Makes a fine hedge or topiary. Dwarf, blue-leaved, and white- or yellow-variegated cultivars are available.

Calycanthus floridus　　　　　Calycanthaceae

CAROLINA ALLSPICE

Plant Carolina allspice near a doorway or window where you can enjoy the fragrance of the flowers. For variety, try the cultivar 'Athens', which has yellow flowers.

SEASON OF INTEREST: Even if you don't see them, you'll enjoy the strawberry fragrance of the flowers from their peak of bloom in spring into summer. The reddish brown flowers hide amid the foliage.

BEST CLIMATE AND SITE: Zones 4–9, though it may die back to older wood or its roots during cold winters in the colder part of this range. Deep, moist, but not wet, soil. Growth is more compact on a sunny site, but the plant will also grow in shade.

GROWING GUIDELINES: Water during drought. Mulch with compost. In early spring, prune off dead wood and awkward long branches.

PEST AND DISEASE PREVENTION: Plants are generally problem-free.

LANDSCAPE USE: Height 6–8 feet (1.8–2.4 m). Some plants stay fairly narrow; others are spreading— plan accordingly. Use in a shrub garden, possibly combined with laurels (*Kalmia* spp.), azaleas (*Rhododendron* spp.) or summersweet (*Clethra alnifolia*). Or set it near your deck or an open window where you can enjoy the fragrance.

OTHER COMMENTS: Not all plants are equally fragrant—try to sniff the flowers before you buy.

RELATED PLANTS:

　PALE SWEETSHRUB (*C. fertilis*): Bears reddish brown flowers without fragrance.

Camellia sasanqua　　　　　Theaceae

SASANQUA CAMELLIA

Add fall or winter interest to a warm-climate garden with late-blooming sasanqua camellia. The showy flowers bloom in a range of colors over the evergreen foliage.

SEASON OF INTEREST: Large pink, red, white, or lavender flowers in the fall. Some cultivars such as 'Shishi Gashira' and 'Yuletide' flower in winter. Foliage is evergreen.

BEST CLIMATE AND SITE: Zones 7–8, but the flower buds are only reliably hardy in the southern part of Zone 8. Protected site with full sun will result in the best flowering and most compact growth. In hot areas, provide afternoon shade. For protection from early fall frosts, plant near a warm wall. Rich, moist, and well-drained acid soil.

GROWING GUIDELINES: Add organic matter to the planting area. Plant in raised beds on poorly drained or heavy soil. Mulch with compost each spring. Water when you get less than 1 inch (25 mm) of rain a week. Prune to shape after flowering.

PEST AND DISEASE PREVENTION: Avoid scale by keeping the plant healthy and vigorous; treat scale attacks with light horticultural oil.

LANDSCAPE USE: Height averages 4–6 feet (1.2–1.8 m), but can grow to 15 feet (4.5 m). If you are willing to prune, you can use one or more in a foundation planting. Or let single specimens reach full height in a garden away from the house. Camellias also make attractive hedges.

RELATED PLANTS:

　COMMON CAMELLIA (*C. japonica*): Tends to be less hardy and have larger flowers.

Carpinus betulus   Betulaceae

EUROPEAN HORNBEAM

Trouble-free European hornbeam is a great shade tree for a medium-sized to large yard. The dark green leaves are rarely bothered by serious pests or diseases.

SEASON OF INTEREST: Dangling catkins in early spring, interesting double-toothed leaves in summer, and yellow foliage in fall. The handsome trunks of this shade tree look muscled beneath smooth gray bark.

BEST CLIMATE AND SITE: Zones 5–9. Full sun; well-drained soil but tolerates slightly light or heavy soil.

GROWING GUIDELINES: Plant small trees in early spring to minimize transplanting difficulties. Mulch and keep grass off the rooting area. Water during drought.

PEST AND DISEASE PREVENTION: Plants are generally problem-free.

LANDSCAPE USE: Height 40–60 feet (12–18 m); width 30–40 feet (9–12 m). Nice shade trees with durable wood that resists damage from wind and ice.

OTHER COMMENTS: Look for 'Pendula', with weeping branches; 'Asplenifolia', with deeply toothed leaves; or 'Purpurea', with purple leaves.

RELATED PLANTS:

AMERICAN HORNBEAM (*C. caroliniana*): Height to 30 feet (9 m) in partial shade. Smooth gray bark that appears to be rippled. Hardy to Zone 2.

Cercidiphyllum japonicum   Cercidiphyllaceae

KATSURA TREE

If you have the space, a katsura tree is one of the most beautiful trees you can grow. In fall, its heart-shaped leaves turn bright colors and are often sweetly scented.

SEASON OF INTEREST: Heart-shaped leaves are interesting during the growing season. The furrowed, shaggy bark is attractive year-round. In fall, the leaves turn yellow, red, or orange and often smell sweet.

BEST CLIMATE AND SITE: Zones 4–8. Full sun; rich, moist, well-drained soil. If exposed to drought, high winds, or high temperatures, the leaves may turn brown and drop.

GROWING GUIDELINES: Plant small, container-grown trees in spring to minimize transplanting difficulties. Mulch regularly. Water during drought. Keep a grass-free area over the root zone.

PEST AND DISEASE PREVENTION: Plants are generally problem-free.

LANDSCAPE USE: Height 50–80 feet (15–24 m); width 30–50 feet (9–15 m). Use as a shade tree.

| *Chamaecyparis obtusa* | Cupressaceae | *Chionanthus virginicus* | Oleaceae |

HINOKI FALSE CYPRESS

WHITE FRINGE TREE

Evergreen Hinoki false cypress thrives in evenly moist soil. Plant in full sun in cool climates; give it a site with a few hours of shade in warmer areas.

White fringe tree thrives in light shade and moist soil. Showy white flower clusters cover the large shrub or small tree in spring; in fall, the leaves turn bright yellow.

SEASON OF INTEREST: Small scale-like leaves are compressed into fan-shaped branches that arch down from a tall slender tree. Some forms are more compact or have golden foliage.

BEST CLIMATE AND SITE: Zones 5–8. Moist but well-drained soil. In a cool climate with ample rainfall, set the plant in full sun; in hot climates, give it a couple hours of afternoon shade. Protect from wind.

GROWING GUIDELINES: Start with container-grown plants to minimize transplanting problems. Mulch well in dry soil, but use less mulch on moist soil; the tree struggles in wet soil.

PEST AND DISEASE PREVENTION: Plant in well-drained soil to avoid root rot.

LANDSCAPE USE: Height 50–75 feet (15–25 m); width 10–30 feet (3–9 m). Makes a great specimen plant. Use as the focal point of a shrub or flower border. Plant dwarf cultivars such as 30-inch (75 cm) tall 'Kosteri' in rock gardens. Consider the cultivars named below for foundation plantings or shrub borders.

OTHER COMMENTS: 'Nana Gracilis' is more compact. 'Aurea' has golden foliage. 'Nana Lutea' is compact and golden.

RELATED PLANTS:

SAWARA FALSE CYPRESS (*C. pisifera*): Has a similar form with variable foliage.

SEASON OF INTEREST: Covered with billowy white clusters of flowers in spring, just after the leaves have opened. The flowers mature into blue berries that attract birds. In fall, the leaves turn yellow before dropping.

BEST CLIMATE AND SITE: Zones 5–8. Choose a cool planting site with light shade (preferably morning sun) and moist, rich soil.

GROWING GUIDELINES: Will struggle during drought. Keep grass out of the rooting zone. Mulch and water when the soil dries out.

PEST AND DISEASE PREVENTION: Avoid hot, dry sites to prevent spider mites.

LANDSCAPE USE: Can grow as a small tree to a height of about 25 feet (7.5 m) with an equal spread or as a multitrunked shrub. Use as a focal point in your landscape or blend into shrub or flower borders. Try it on the east side of a house or in the sunny openings beneath shade trees. Underplant with groundcovers like English ivy (*Hedera helix*) or spotted lamium (*Lamium maculatum*) cultivars.

RELATED PLANTS:

CHINESE FRINGE TREE (*C. retusus*): Spikes of white flowers in June and July. Height to 20 feet (6 m).

Cladastris lutea   Leguminosae

AMERICAN YELLOWWOOD

Plant an American yellowwood for year-round interest: it features white flowers in late spring to early summer, bright yellow fall color, and handsome, smooth gray bark all year.

SEASON OF INTEREST: Long clusters of fragrant white flowers emerge through the bright green, compound leaves in May and June. The flowers mature to short pods. In the fall, the leaves turn yellow. The gray bark is attractive in winter.

BEST CLIMATE AND SITE: Zones 4–8. Full sun; well-drained soil.

GROWING GUIDELINES: Can develop upright-growing branches that can break off in ice or wind. Shape young trees to make them stronger. Remove side branches that emerge with less than a 45-degree angle from the trunk. Prune during summer; the sap leaks heavily after winter or spring pruning.

PEST AND DISEASE PREVENTION: Plants are generally problem-free.

LANDSCAPE USE: Height 30–50 feet (9–15 m); nearly equal spread. Use as a compact shade tree for small areas or for a shade garden.

Clethra alnifolia   Clethraceae

SUMMERSWEET

Add flowers and fragrance to your summer garden with a planting of summersweet. This moisture-loving but adaptable shrub will tolerate heavy shade and even wet soil.

SEASON OF INTEREST: Sends out spiky clusters of small but fragrant white flowers in midsummer; they'll bloom for up to 6 weeks. Leaves are bright yellow or orange in fall.

BEST CLIMATE AND SITE: Zones 5–9. Grows in sun or shade; thrives in moist, organic-rich soil with a moderately acid pH; tolerates wet soil.

GROWING GUIDELINES: Keep the soil moist; add extra organic matter to the planting bed and mulch regularly. In early spring, remove lanky or old branches down to the base or to a side branch to encourage more new growth and flowers.

PEST AND DISEASE PREVENTION: Avoid dry sites to prevent spider mites.

LANDSCAPE USE: Height 3–8 feet (90–240 cm); slightly narrower spread. May be too tall for a foundation planting, unless you prune regularly, but you can use it in woodland or shade gardens or in ornamental gardens with sweet bay (*Magnolia virginiana*) and inkberry (*Ilex glabra*). Or try it near water or protected seaside locations.

OTHER COMMENTS: 'Rosea' has pink flower buds; 'Paniculata' has larger flower clusters.

RELATED PLANTS:

CINNAMON CLETHRA (*C. acuminata*): Grows into a small tree or shrub; height to 18 feet (5.4 m). Bears similar fragrant flowers in late July.

KOUSA DOGWOOD

REDVEIN ENKIANTHUS

Easy-care kousa dogwood is covered with flower-like white bracts in early summer, followed by dangling reddish fruits. The leaves of this small tree turn red in fall.

SEASON OF INTEREST: Begins flowering in early June, several weeks after the native flowering dogwood (*Cornus florida*). Bears tiered layers of white bracts that resemble flowers. You'll enjoy the orange to red berries in summer and the red foliage in the fall.

BEST CLIMATE AND SITE: Zones 5–8. Full sun in cool climates or a couple hours of afternoon shade in hot climates; rich, acid, well-drained soil.

GROWING GUIDELINES: Enrich the planting bed with organic matter before planting. Mulch regularly. Water during drought.

PEST AND DISEASE PREVENTION: Avoid hot or dry locations to prevent borers.

LANDSCAPE USE: Height to 20 feet (6 m); nearly equal spread. Use to soften the corners of buildings, but provide enough room for the branches to spread, and avoid hot southern or western exposures. Include kousa dogwood in a mixed flower garden or shrub border or make it a focal point near a patio or paved area.

RELATED PLANTS:

FLOWERING DOGWOOD (*C. florida*): Grows best in light shade; bears white or pink, bract-like flowers in May. Susceptible to borers and anthracnose in some areas.

Redvein enkianthus thrives in sun to light shade, with acid soil that is evenly moist but well drained. If your site has wet or heavy soil, plant in raised beds instead.

SEASON OF INTEREST: Small, yellow, urn-shaped flowers with red veins appear with new leaves in May. The foliage turns bright red or orange in the fall.

BEST CLIMATE AND SITE: Zones 5–9. Full sun or light shade; acid, moist, well-drained soil. Tolerates dense shade but flowers less.

GROWING GUIDELINES: Plant in raised beds in heavy or wet soil. Mulch regularly.

PEST AND DISEASE PREVENTION: Plants are generally problem-free.

LANDSCAPE USE: Height 6–8 feet (1.8–2.4 m) in cold climates; grows to 30 feet (9 m) in warm climates. Use near a walk or patio where you can see the flowers up close. Or plant it in a shrub border with rhododendrons (*Rhododendron* spp.) and spotted lamium (*Lamium maculatum*).

| *Euonymus alata* | Celastraceae | *Forsythia* x *intermedia* | Oleaceae |

BURNING BUSH

BORDER FORSYTHIA

Light up your late-season landscape with the glowing scarlet fall color of burning bush. The species grows large, so give it room to spread or choose a compact cultivar.

SEASON OF INTEREST: Handsome, horizontally spreading branches and a neat rounded shape are attractive year-round. Vibrant, scarlet fall color.

BEST CLIMATE AND SITE: Zones 3–9. Sun to medium shade; well-drained soil.

GROWING GUIDELINES: Choose compact cultivars for smaller areas so you won't have to prune. Water during drought.

PEST AND DISEASE PREVENTION: Avoid hot, dry sites to prevent spider mites. Prune and destroy parts infested by scale.

LANDSCAPE USE: Height 10–20 feet (3–6 m). Too large for a foundation planting. Use for a hedge, screen, or shrub grouping.

OTHER COMMENTS: The dwarf winged euonymus (*E. alata* 'Compactus') will mature at a height of about 10 feet (3 m).

RELATED PLANTS:

WINTERCREEPER (*E. fortunei*): A low-growing groundcover species; see the entry on page 50.

The yellow flowers of border forsythia are a common sight in spring. Space plants so they have room to spread—they'll have a nicer form and will need minimal pruning.

SEASON OF INTEREST: Brief but exciting display of glowing, yellow-gold flowers in spring.

BEST CLIMATE AND SITE: Zones 5–9, although the flower buds on most cultivars are only hardy to Zone 6. Full sun; soil that is not overly wet or dry.

GROWING GUIDELINES: Prune after flowering. Thin out older or particularly upright branches; leave those that gently cascade.

PEST AND DISEASE PREVENTION: Plants are generally problem-free.

LANDSCAPE USE: Height to 10 feet (3 m); width to 12 feet (3.6 m). Too tall for a foundation planting. Use where it has room to spread, in an informal hedge or screen, on a bank, or in a shrub border.

OTHER COMMENTS: The hybrid 'Meadowlark' has extra hardy flower buds and is a good choice for Northern climates.

RELATED PLANTS:

BRONX GREENSTEM FORSYTHIA (*F. virdissima* 'Bronxensis'): Height to 1 foot (30 cm); produces typical golden forsythia flowers on bright green stems.

WEEPING FORSYTHIA (*F. suspensa*): Bears golden flowers in early spring on cascading branches up to 10 feet (3 m) long.

Fothergilla gardenii Hamamelidaceae	*Halesia carolina* Styracaceae

DWARF FOTHERGILLA

CAROLINA SILVERBELL

Dwarf fothergilla is a small shrub whose pom-pom-like flowers are a welcome sight in spring. The leathery leaves turn brilliant yellow, orange, and scarlet in fall.

Carolina silverbell likes extra organic matter at planting and later as a mulch. But it's worth the effort when the white, bell-shaped flowers decorate the tree in spring.

SEASON OF INTEREST: Fragrant white flowers that look like bottle brushes appear in late April and early May before the leaves. The leathery, dark green leaves turn yellow, orange, and scarlet— sometimes all on each leaf— in the fall.

BEST CLIMATE AND SITE: Zones 5–9. Full sun for more flowers and better fall color; provide afternoon shade in warmer climates. Acid, well-drained, moist soil.

GROWING GUIDELINES: Water when the soil begins to dry out.

PEST AND DISEASE PREVENTION: Plants are generally problem-free.

LANDSCAPE USE: Height and spread 2–3 feet (60–90 cm). Use in foundation plantings, in front of leggy evergreens, amid flowers, or in masses. Combine with rhododendrons and azaleas (*Rhododendron* spp.) and redvein enkianthus (*Enkianthus campanulatus*).

RELATED PLANTS:

LARGE FOTHERGILLA (*F. major*): Similar white flowers in spring and striking multiple leaf colors in fall. Height to 10 feet (3 m).

SEASON OF INTEREST: Dainty, white bell-shaped flowers dangle beneath the branches in April and early May. The foliage turns yellow early in the fall.

BEST CLIMATE AND SITE: Zones 5–8. Morning sun with a few hours of afternoon shade; acid, moist, well-drained, fertile soil.

GROWING GUIDELINES: Prepare the planting bed with extra organic matter. Mulch with compost every spring. Water during drought. Keep grass off the rooting area.

PEST AND DISEASE PREVENTION: Plants are generally problem-free.

LANDSCAPE USE: Height 30–40 feet (9–12 m). Use near a patio or walkway where you can see the flowers from below. Or try it in shrub borders, at the edge of woodlands, or amid rhododendrons (*Rhododendron* spp.).

RELATED PLANTS:

MOUNTAIN SILVERBELL (*H. monticola*): Height to 80 feet (24 m); bears flowers that are slightly longer than Carolina silverbell. 'Rosea' has pink flowers.

| *Hibiscus syriacus* | Malvaceae | *Hydrangea quercifolia* | Hydrangeaceae |

ROSE-OF-SHARON

OAK-LEAVED HYDRANGEA

Shrubby rose-of-Sharon bears hibiscus-like flowers in summer. Look for cultivars that set little or no seed to avoid hundreds of self-sown seedlings in your yard.

Oak-leaved hydrangea is a handsome shrub for moist, acid soil. Enjoy the huge flower clusters in summer, the deep red color in fall, and the peeling bark in winter.

SEASON OF INTEREST: Provides a riot of summer color with blue-purple, white, or red flowers up to 4 inches (10 cm) wide. The three-lobed leaves make a nice backdrop for the flowers.

BEST CLIMATE AND SITE: Zones 5–9. Preferably full sun; can take a few hours of shade but may not bloom as heavily. Moist, well-drained, rich soil.

GROWING GUIDELINES: Since it flowers on new growth, prune the main branches back to 6–8 inches (15–20 cm) in early spring. Then encourage growth by fertilizing once or twice a season with a complete organic fertilizer—one with similar percentages of nitrogen, phosphorus, and potassium—or compost. You may need to trim long branches in summer to keep it from outgrowing its space. Water during drought.

PEST AND DISEASE PREVENTION: Avoid hot, dry locations to prevent spider mites. Treat aphids clustering on new shoots with insecticidal soap.

LANDSCAPE USE: Height 8–10 feet (2.4–3 m); width 6–10 feet (1.8–3 m). This flashy shrub makes an excellent patio plant or bright spot in a shrub border or flower bed.

OTHER COMMENTS: Self-sown seedlings can be a problem. Look for cultivars that produce little or no seed, such as 'Aphrodite', 'Diana', 'Helene', and 'Minerva'.

SEASON OF INTEREST: Provides changing highlights through the growing season. Handsome, flat-topped, white flower clusters in June fade to purple and brown during summer. In the fall, the large lobed leaves turn maroon before they drop.

BEST CLIMATE AND SITE: Zones 5–9. Tolerates light shade, but will flower best in full sun if you keep the roots cool and moist. Moist, well-drained, fertile, acid soil.

GROWING GUIDELINES: Mulch regularly. Prune after flowering, if necessary. Remove dead wood anytime.

PEST AND DISEASE PREVENTION: Plants are generally problem-free.

LANDSCAPE USE: Height 4–6 feet (1.2–1.8 m); width 3–5 feet (90–150 m). Makes an attractive and compact foundation plant. Or use in shrub borders, around woodland edges, or in a mixed flower bed for height.

OTHER COMMENTS: 'Harmony' and 'Snowflake' have larger flower clusters.

RELATED PLANTS:

GARDEN HYDRANGEA (*H. macrophylla*): Height to 8 feet (2.4 m); bears pink or blue flowers.

PEEGEE HYDRANGEA (*H. paniculata* 'Grandiflora'): Height 15–25 feet (4.5–7.5 m). Bears white flower clusters up to 8 inches (20 cm) across.

Ilex crenata Aquifoliaceae	*Kalmia latifolia* Ericaceae

JAPANESE HOLLY

MOUNTAIN LAUREL

Evergreen Japanese holly can vary widely in height, depending on the cultivar. Plant tall forms for hedges; use compact forms for easy-care foundation plantings.

SEASON OF INTEREST: Attractive year-round. Some cultivars develop purple leaves during winter.

BEST CLIMATE AND SITE: Zones 5–8. Full sun; well-drained, acid soil.

GROWING GUIDELINES: Shear it as needed or buy low-growing cultivars that need no trimming.

PEST AND DISEASE PREVENTION: Plants are generally problem-free.

LANDSCAPE USE: Cultivars such as 'Helleri' grow to 1½ feet (40 cm) tall; 'Hetzii' swells up to 6 feet (1.8 m) high, and 'Rotundifolia' stretches to 10 feet (3 m) high. Use compact cultivars for foundation plantings or flower borders; plant taller cultivars as hedges or screens.

RELATED PLANTS:

INKBERRY (*I. glabra*): Height and spread to 8 feet (2.4 m). Hardier than Japanese holly; small, oval, evergreen leaves.

Mountain laurel thrives in cool climates, on sites with evenly moist, well-drained soil. It flowers best in sun, but it can be beautiful in the shade garden, too.

SEASON OF INTEREST: Clusters of fragrant flowers— shallow trumpets of white or pink with darker rose markings—in June. Some cultivars have flower buds with contrasting colors. Evergreen leaves are attractive all year.

BEST CLIMATE AND SITE: Zones 4–7. Flowers best in full sun if the roots are cool but tolerates medium shade; moist, well-drained, acid soil.

GROWING GUIDELINES: Thin out older branches to encourage new growth and more flowers. Or preserve the older branches to give the shrub an open, sculpted look. Deadhead after flowering. Mulch with compost every year.

PEST AND DISEASE PREVENTION: Plants are generally problem-free.

LANDSCAPE USE: Height to 15 feet (4.5 m). If you don't want to prune regularly, give them room to ramble in a shrub border or woodland edge.

RELATED PLANTS:

SHEEP LAUREL (*K. angustifolia*): Hardy to Zone 2. Height 1–3 feet (30–90 cm); has purple flowers.

Kerria japonica   Rosaceae

JAPANESE KERRIA

The sunny yellow blooms of Japanese kerria light up the shady garden in spring and often appear sporadically through the season. In winter, enjoy the colorful stems.

SEASON OF INTEREST: Produces a profusion of bright yellow flowers, reminiscent of roses, in spring. They are followed by bright green leaves that drop in fall to reveal yellow to green winter stems.

BEST CLIMATE AND SITE: Zones 5–8. Light shade; well-drained soil of average fertility. Tolerates short periods of summer drought; may begin to flower when rain returns.

GROWING GUIDELINES: Prune after flowering to remove any overly long or straggly stems. Mulch with compost every year.

PEST AND DISEASE PREVENTION: Avoid wet soil to prevent root rot. To escape leaf spots, provide good air circulation and clean up fallen leaves. To avoid stem cankers, keep the plant growing vigorously and be careful you don't damage the bark with lawn tools. If stem cankers strike, cut them out.

LANDSCAPE USE: Height 3–6 feet (90–180 cm); slightly wider spread. Use in a foundation planting or a flower garden. Mass in a shrub border or cluster in front of taller plants.

OTHER COMMENTS: 'Aureo-variegata' has variegated leaves; 'Aureo-vittata' has striped stems; 'Pleniflora' has double flowers.

Magnolia stellata   Magnoliaceae

STAR MAGNOLIA

Star magnolia is a beautiful, easy-care large shrub or small tree. Set plants on a slope and avoid south-facing exposures to prevent flowers from damage by late frosts.

SEASON OF INTEREST: Welcomes spring with a magnificent show of fragrant white flowers in early April. Through the rest of the growing season it has clean foliage, furry buds, and a graceful branching pattern.

BEST CLIMATE AND SITE: Zones 5–9. Full sun or light shade; moist, rich, slightly acid soil. Protect from spring frosts. Avoid the southern side of the house or a south-facing bank or the flowers will open even earlier and be more frost-susceptible. Set it halfway up a slope to escape frosts that can linger at the bottom and winds that sweep at the top.

GROWING GUIDELINES: Enrich the planting area with plenty of organic matter. Move younger plants in spring to minimize transplanting difficulties. Mulch regularly.

PEST AND DISEASE PREVENTION: Plants are generally problem-free.

LANDSCAPE USE: Height 15–20 feet (4.5–6 m); slightly less spread. Multistemmed shrub form grows to a height of about 12 feet (3.6 m). Use either form outside the corner of a building, as a focal point in a garden, near a patio, or in a shrub or flower border.

RELATED PLANTS:

SAUCER MAGNOLIA (_M._ x _soulangiana_): Height to 20 feet (6 m). Big white flowers in spring.

Mahonia aquifolium   Berberidaceae

OREGON GRAPE

If you have a shady spot with moist, acid soil, try a planting of Oregon grape. This glossy evergreen shrub is topped with clusters of fragrant yellow flowers in spring.

SEASON OF INTEREST: Produces long clusters of sweetly fragrant, yellow flowers in April. In summer, they mature into dark blue grape-like berries that may stay on the plant into late fall (if the birds don't eat them). The long, glossy, evergreen leaves, actually a collection of toothed leaflets, take on a purplish tint in winter.

BEST CLIMATE AND SITE: Zones 5–9; extra hardy cultivars can survive in Zone 5. Medium shade; cool, moist, acid soil. Too much sun or winter wind will make the leaf edges brown.

GROWING GUIDELINES: Enrich the planting bed with plenty of organic matter. Mulch regularly. Water during drought.

PEST AND DISEASE PREVENTION: Plants are generally problem-free.

LANDSCAPE USE: Height 3–6 feet (90–180 cm); width 3–8 feet (90–240 cm), depending on whether the stems are upright or arching. Use as a foundation plant, in a shrub border, or in a shade garden.

Nandina domestica   Berberidaceae

HEAVENLY BAMBOO

Heavenly bamboo is a favorite of warm-climate gardeners for its fine-textured evergreen leaves, white flower clusters in spring, and red berries in fall and winter.

SEASON OF INTEREST: This broad-leaved evergreen has colorful dark or blue-green foliage if you grow it in shade and light green to reddish foliage if you grow it in full sun. Each leaf is twice or thrice compound, giving the appearance of a bamboo leaf. Produces clusters of small white flowers in spring. The flowers turn into bright red berries that you'll enjoy in fall and winter, especially if they are displayed against the blue-green foliage of shade-grown plants.

BEST CLIMATE AND SITE: Zones 6–10. Sun or shade; tolerates any cool soil.

GROWING GUIDELINES: Easy to grow and tolerant of drought. Fertilize lightly and cool the soil with mulch. Thin older stems to encourage new growth.

PEST AND DISEASE PREVENTION: Plants are generally problem-free.

LANDSCAPE USE: Height 5–7 feet (1.5–2.1 m); width to 5 feet (1.5 m). Use as a foundation plant or in a shrub border

OTHER COMMENTS: The red berries are poisonous; keep young children away.

Parrotia persica   Hamamelidaceae   *Picea omorika*   Pinaceae

PERSIAN PARROTIA

Add a distinctive touch to your landscape with colorful Persian parrotia. It has particularly striking red, orange, or yellow fall color and showy peeling bark.

SEASON OF INTEREST: Flashy, fiery red stamens do the job of petals when parrotia bursts into bloom in April. A month later, the red-tinted foliage unfurls. The leaves change to medium green for summer and then to red, orange, or yellow in the fall. During winter, you'll enjoy the peeling brown, gray, green, and white trunk bark.

BEST CLIMATE AND SITE: Zones 5–9. Does best in full sun, but can tolerate a few hours of shade; rich, well-drained, slightly acid soil.

GROWING GUIDELINES: Enrich the planting bed with organic matter.

PEST AND DISEASE PREVENTION: Plants are generally problem-free.

LANDSCAPE USE: Tree form height to 40 feet (12 m); slightly narrower spread. Multistemmed shrub height to 20 feet (6 m). Put either form where you can see the changing colors through the seasons. Use for shade, as a street tree, or in a shrub border. Or make it part of a flower border—pick up the color of the new leaves with red tulips; set off the fall colors with gold, orange, and red chrysanthemums.

SERBIAN SPRUCE

Adaptable Serbian spruce is a particularly handsome evergreen for a large yard. It has a narrow, pyramidal habit and glossy green needles that are silvery underneath.

SEASON OF INTEREST: Attractive year-round; has an elegant upright shape with gently cascading branches. The forest green needles are silver underneath. The cones reach 2½ inches (7.5 cm) long.

BEST CLIMATE AND SITE: Zones 5–8. Light shade; well-drained, moist soil. Protect from winter winds.

GROWING GUIDELINES: Give Serbian spruce room to stretch up to its full height and width so that you will not have to prune it.

PEST AND DISEASE PREVENTION: Plants are generally problem-free.

LANDSCAPE USE: Height 60 feet (18 m) or more; width 25 feet (7.5 m). Blend with pines, spruces, or firs of different colors to make an attractive evergreen screen. Or use a lone Serbian spruce at the edge of a woodland or grove of shade trees for winter color.

OTHER COMMENTS: 'Nana', a dwarf form, grows to about 15 feet (4.5 m) tall.

RELATED PLANTS:

COLORADO SPRUCE (*P. pungens*): Bluish or green needles; height to 100 feet (30 m); may become rangy with age.

NORWAY SPRUCE (*P. abies*): Dangling young branches; height to 50 feet (15 m) or more.

ORIENTAL SPRUCE (*P. orientalis*): Small needles; height to 60 feet (18 m).

Pieris floribunda   Ericaceae   *Pinus thunbergiana*   Pinaceae

MOUNTAIN PIERIS

JAPANESE BLACK PINE

Spiky clusters of white flowers highlight this rounded, bushy shrub in spring. Try evergreen mountain pieris in a flower border with bulbs for early color.

Japanese black pine is a tough, adaptable evergreen tree for sunny, well-drained sites. It is a great choice for seaside plantings, since it is quite salt-tolerant.

SEASON OF INTEREST: Short clusters of urn-shaped white flowers in April. They stand above attractive, glossy evergreen leaves.

BEST CLIMATE AND SITE: Zones 5–8. Sun or light shade; well-drained, acid to neutral soil. Avoid warm, southern exposures that encourage early flowering and increase the risk of frost damage.

GROWING GUIDELINES: Add plenty of organic matter to the bed before planting. Mulch regularly. Deadhead after flowering.

PEST AND DISEASE PREVENTION: Plants are generally problem-free.

LANDSCAPE USE: Height 2–6 feet (60–180 cm); similar spread. Versatile enough to use in your foundation planting, in the front of a shrub border, in a mixed flower garden amid early crocuses and daffodils, or in a broad-leaved evergreen garden with rhododendrons and azaleas (*Rhododendron* spp.).

RELATED PLANTS:

JAPANESE PIERIS (*P. japonica*): Grows up to twice as tall as mountain pieris and flowers earlier. Requires light shade. Prone to leaf damage from lacebugs.

SEASON OF INTEREST: Interesting year-round; glossy needles are 3–7 inches (7.5–17.5 cm) long and bundled together in pairs. Grows into an open, roughly triangular shape, providing welcome variety from the symmetrical conical shape of many conifers. The dark bark is given character by deep fissures.

BEST CLIMATE AND SITE: Zones 5–8. Can suffer disfiguring dieback during severe winters. Full sun; well-drained, moist, fertile soil. Tolerates sandy soil and salt exposure.

GROWING GUIDELINES: Fertile soil will help the tree grow faster but possibly lankier. In exposed areas, limit soil fertility to make the tree denser and stronger.

PEST AND DISEASE PREVENTION: Enrich the planting bed with organic matter and mulch regularly to avoid pine nematodes in the eastern United States.

LANDSCAPE USE: Height 30–70 feet (9–21 m) depending on the site and the genetics of the particular plant. The mature spread averages about half of the height but can differ with each tree. Use in groups as a screen or individually in informal gardens or naturalized areas. Set near sand dunes or shorelines to stabilize the soil and protect areas inland from salt and wind.

Potentilla fruticosa Rosaceae

SHRUBBY CINQUEFOIL

Easy-to-grow shrubby cinquefoil is a great choice for adding color to your yard from early summer to frost. This tough plant needs little pruning and can take poor, dry soil.

SEASON OF INTEREST: Yellow, orange, or white flowers in summer and fall.

BEST CLIMATE AND SITE: Zones 2–8; thrives in Zones 3–5. Full sun for the best flowering, but light shade in hot and humid areas; well-drained, sandy, saline, or nutrient-poor soil.

GROWING GUIDELINES: Usually grows into a loose mound shape that needs little pruning. Shorten or remove individual branches that protrude.

PEST AND DISEASE PREVENTION: Plants are generally problem-free.

LANDSCAPE USE: Height 1–4 feet (30–120 cm); similar spread. Add one or several to a perennial border, foundation planting, or shrub bed. Mass more into a low hedge or visual barrier dividing one part of the landscape from another. You could combine it with creeping juniper (*Juniperus horizontalis*) and the pink, orange, and yellow flowers of rose moss (*Portulaca grandiflora*).

RELATED PLANTS: See the Three-toothed cinquefoil (*P. tridentata*) entry on page 55.

Pseudotsuga menziesii Pinaceae

DOUGLAS FIR

Evergreen Douglas fir thrives in cool, humid climates, on a site with moist but well-drained soil. Try it as a specimen or plant it in masses for a tall screen.

SEASON OF INTEREST: This strong, tall conifer is beautiful year-round. The needles of the hardiest strains are blue-green; the less hardy strain is soft green.

BEST CLIMATE AND SITE: Zones 4–7. Full sun; deep, cool, moist, well-drained soil. Provide shelter from high winds.

GROWING GUIDELINES: Native to cool mountain climates. If you grow it in Zone 6 or 7, mulch to keep the soil as cool as possible. Mature trees can tolerate a short drought, but you'll have to water younger trees.

PEST AND DISEASE PREVENTION: Site the plant in its preferred conditions to avoid pest and disease problems such as cankers, blights, aphids, and scale.

LANDSCAPE USE: Height 100 feet (30 m); width 20–30 feet (6–9 m). Use where it has room to stretch up tall and slim. Group several into a screen for large yards. Or mix one or two in a wooded grove with hemlocks (*Tsuga* spp.), oaks (*Quercus* spp.), and rhododendrons (*Rhododendron* spp.).

RHODODENDRONS

Rhododendrons and azaleas are popular landscape plants for their showy spring or summer flowers. They'll thrive in light shade and acid soil; good drainage is a must.

SEASON OF INTEREST: Most rhododendrons bloom in late spring or early summer, but a few bloom from July into August. They bear bold bell-shaped flowers, sometimes massed into clusters. The main flower colors are pink, white, and lavender, but you also can find reds, yellows, and purples. The glossy evergreen foliage is handsome year-round.

BEST CLIMATE AND SITE: If you pick cultivars well suited for your area, you can grow rhododendrons from Zones 4–9. For most types, provide light shade, preferably with morning sun. It's essential that you provide well-drained, acid soil (pH of 4.5–6.5) rich in organic matter.

GROWING GUIDELINES: Prepare the planting bed with plenty of organic matter. Raise it if necessary to improve drainage. Mulch with compost or leaf mold. Water during drought.

PEST AND DISEASE PREVENTION: Provide well-drained soil to prevent root or stem rot. Stay away from hot, dry sites to discourage spider mites.

LANDSCAPE USE: Rhododendron hybrids come in all sizes and shapes. Tree forms can grow to 25 feet (7.5 m); rock garden plants may only reach 2 feet (60 cm). Use as a tall accent or sweep of low color in a shade garden, include them in flower gardens, or plant as an informal hedge or screen.

RELATED PLANTS: The genus *Rhododendron* also includes azaleas, which require similar conditions.

RUGOSA ROSE

If you're looking for an easy-care rose, rugosa rose is for you! Enjoy the colorful flowers and dark green leaves in summer and the large, bright red fruit in fall.

SEASON OF INTEREST: A dense, thorny bush producing pink, rose, or white flowers in abundance in early summer and occasionally afterward. The flowers are followed by bright red seedpods, called rosehips.

BEST CLIMATE AND SITE: Zones 3–8. Full sun; for best performance, well-drained soil that is rich in organic matter, preferably with a slightly acid pH. Tolerates dry, sandy, and saline soil; great for seaside gardens.

GROWING GUIDELINES: Side-dress with compost in spring. Remove old canes; wear gloves to avoid scratches.

PEST AND DISEASE PREVENTION: Plants are generally problem-free.

LANDSCAPE USE: Height 4–6 feet (1.2–1.8 m); similar spread. Blend into shrub or flower borders, or use as a prickly hedge that people and pests won't dare push through. Or let them colonize difficult sites like banks and beaches.

Stephanandra incisa   Rosaceae

LACE SHRUB

Lovely lace shrub bears gracefully arching branches clad in finely cut bright green leaves. Give it moist soil, sun or light shade, and plenty of room for it to spread.

SEASON OF INTEREST: Fine-textured leaves steal the show; they open warm red, mature to bright green, and then turn red-purple or orange in fall.

BEST CLIMATE AND SITE: Zones 4–8. Full sun for best results; tolerates light shade. Moist, well-drained soil enriched with organic matter. Protect from wind to keep the younger shoots from dying back.

GROWING GUIDELINES: Allow plenty of open space for the plant to roam—it roots anywhere its arching branches meet the ground. Container-grown plants will transplant most easily. Prune in early spring, removing any dead or damaged branches.

PEST AND DISEASE PREVENTION: Plants are generally problem-free.

LANDSCAPE USE: Height to 5 feet (1.5 m); similar spread. It's great for anywhere you want a big sweep of greenery—on a bank, in a border, over an unused corner of the yard, or in hedge or screen.

OTHER COMMENTS: The cultivar 'Crispa' grows to 2 feet (60 cm) tall.

Stewartia pseudocamellia   Theaceae

JAPANESE STEWARTIA

Plant Japanese stewartia for its beautiful peeling bark, white summer flowers, and yellow, reddish, or purplish fall color. It's a distinctive addition to any landscape.

SEASON OF INTEREST: Produces lovely white flowers in summer and early fall. They are followed by vivid fall leaf colors. You'll especially enjoy the peeling red bark during winter.

BEST CLIMATE AND SITE: Zones 5–9. Light shade; moist, rich, acid soil (pH of 4.5–5.5).

GROWING GUIDELINES: Limit transplanting difficulties by moving small, container-grown plants in early spring. Mulch after planting. Water during drought.

PEST AND DISEASE PREVENTION: Plants are generally problem-free.

LANDSCAPE USE: Height 40–60 feet (12–18 m). Use as a landscape focal point. Make it a shade tree or the highlight at the edge of a shady grove. Or combine it in a mixed planting with broad-leaved evergreens.

RELATED PLANTS:

KOREAN STEWARTIA (*S. koreana*): Height to 20 feet (6 m); has slightly larger flowers and orange, gray, and brown bark.

Styrax japonicus   Styracaceae

JAPANESE SNOWBELL

Graceful Japanese snowbell is an excellent, easy-care small tree for almost every yard. Plant it on a slope so you can see the white flowers that hang down from the branches.

SEASON OF INTEREST: Small clusters of white or pink, bell-shaped flowers about 1 inch (2.5 cm) long dangle amid leaves in June. They are followed in late summer by gray berries and in fall by yellow or red leaves. The smooth bark is colored with orangish fissures.

BEST CLIMATE AND SITE: Zones 5–9. Sun or light shade; moist, well-drained, acid soil rich in organic matter.

GROWING GUIDELINES: Enrich the planting bed with extra organic matter. Transplant young plants in early spring. Water during drought and mulch regularly.

PEST AND DISEASE PREVENTION: Plants are generally problem-free.

LANDSCAPE USE: Height to 30 feet (9 m). Use near a path, drive, or patio where you can enjoy the blooms and berries from below.

Taxus cuspidata   Taxaceae

JAPANESE YEW

Japanese yew can adapt to sun or light shade, but it must have well-drained soil. Though they will take heavy pruning, the plants have a more natural look when left untrimmed.

SEASON OF INTEREST: Evergreen Japanese yews have short, flat, needle-like leaves. If you have both male and female plants, the females will bear red berries in summer.

BEST CLIMATE AND SITE: Zones 5–7. Sun to medium shade; intense winter sun and wind can cause the leaves to brown. Well-drained, moist soil of average fertility.

GROWING GUIDELINES: Plant in raised beds if your soil is heavy or poorly drained. Shear as often as necessary to maintain as a formal hedge. Or use plants individually or in small groups and let them keep a soft, natural look. Prune once a year, removing any overly long branches at the base or at a side branch. To avoid pruning, plant dwarf cultivars.

PEST AND DISEASE PREVENTION: Plant only in well-drained soil to avoid root rot.

LANDSCAPE USE: Height 12–35 feet (3.6–10.5 m); dwarf types such as 'North Coast' or 'Densa' only reach to 4 feet (1.2 m). Use the latter for foundation plantings and taller types for hedges or screens. Group lower growers in masses and on banks.

OTHER COMMENTS: The red berries are poisonous; keep young children away.

RELATED PLANTS:
   ENGLISH YEW (*T. baccata*): Looks similar but hardy in Zones 6–8.

Viburnum plicatum var. *tomentosum*   Caprifoliaceae

DOUBLEFILE VIBURNUM

Doublefile viburnum is an outstanding shrub for the low-maintenance landscape. Its horizontal branches and dark green leaves are topped with white flower clusters in late spring.

SEASON OF INTEREST: Tiers of white flower clusters on horizontally growing branches in May. In summer, dark red berries attract birds. During the fall, the foliage turns a handsome dark red.

BEST CLIMATE AND SITE: Zones 5–8. Sun or light shade; moist, well-drained soil. Be sure to provide at least 4 hours of sun for good flowering and compact growth.

GROWING GUIDELINES: Water during drought. Prune only to remove dead wood. If you shear the plant, you'll destroy its handsome branching structure.

PEST AND DISEASE PREVENTION: Plants are generally problem-free.

LANDSCAPE USE: Height and spread to 10 feet (3 m). To enjoy the branching pattern, give doublefile viburnum room to spread to its full size. Group in shrub borders or use as a backdrop for flower gardens. Try a staggered or straight row as an informal hedge or screen.

Zelkova serrata   Ulmaceae

JAPANESE ZELKOVA

Try Japanese zelkova as a shade tree for a large yard. This stately deciduous tree bears dark green leaves that turn orange, yellow, or reddish in fall.

SEASON OF INTEREST: This handsome shade tree, with its toothed elm-like leaves, looks good through the growing season and into winter. The foliage turns yellow, orange, or red before it drops in fall. The peeling and reddish bark looks good even in winter.

BEST CLIMATE AND SITE: Zones 5–8. Full sun; moist, well-drained soil. Larger plants can tolerate drought.

GROWING GUIDELINES: Protect young trees from wind; water them during drought. Thin out some upright branches while the trees are small to prevent overcrowding.

PEST AND DISEASE PREVENTION: Avoid bark beetles by planting beetle-resistant 'Village Green'.

LANDSCAPE USES: Grows to 80 feet (24 m) tall; perfect for a shade or street tree.

OTHER COMMENTS: The cultivar 'Village Green' has glorious red fall color. The cultivar 'Green Vase' has a graceful vase shape much like the American elm.

RELATED PLANTS:

ELM ZELKOVA (*Z. carpinifolia*): Similar but smaller leaves. Zones 6–9.

QUICK AND COLORFUL
FLOWER GARDENS

To some people, just the mention of low-maintenance landscaping conjures up images of gravel-covered front yards or expanses of boring green groundcovers. But there's no reason that low care has to mean no flowers. With a little planning, you can have "knock-your-socks-off" color and spend a minimum of time on routine maintenance.

Most garden flowers fall into one of three categories. It's handy to understand these three groupings because they'll influence how much and what kind of maintenance you'll need to put into the flowers you grow.

Annuals are plants that live only one growing season. Since the parent plants die off at the end of the season, you need to replace them every year with seeds or transplants. Their strong points are that they're very easy to grow (even if you get a late start in spring planning and planting), they bloom for a long time, and they come in just about any color and height you want.

Hardy perennials come back year after year, so you don't have to buy and replant them each spring. Unlike annuals, most perennials only flower for a short while (days or weeks) each season. But many do offer attractive forms and foliage, so they look almost as good out of bloom as they do in bloom. Most bulbs—including daffodils and crocuses—are also perennials. They go dormant after flowering, freeing up space for annuals or maturing perennial plants.

Biennials live 2 years. The first year they form a rosette of leaves. The second year they send up a flower stalk, blossom, set seed, and die. Some, like pansies, are commonly grown as annuals. Some that reseed easily, like hollyhock (*Alcea rosea*), are as dependable as perennials.

Since it takes some planning and patience to get a good show from most biennials, however, they tend to be grown less frequently than annuals and perennials.

In the garden, you could choose to keep your annuals, biennials, and perennials separated into different beds. But combining them into one glorious garden lets you enjoy the benefits of each kind while minimizing the drawbacks. Early-blooming perennials (like irises and peonies) combine well with annuals like cosmos and cleomes (*Cleome* spp.), which start blooming in early summer and carry on until frost.

Within each group you can find low-maintenance plants. The trick is to choose those that don't need special attention such as staking, indoor winter storage, or frequent pruning. Do look for plants that shrug off heat, scoff at drought, and laugh in the face of pests. Although going the low-maintenance route eliminates some touchy species, you'll still have more to choose from than you could ever hope to grow.

In this chapter, you'll find lots of hints on creating great-looking gardens. "Designing a Low-maintenance Flower Garden" on page 92 gives the basics you'll want to consider when planning your plantings. "Easy Annuals" on page 94 and "Low-maintenance Perennials and Bulbs" on page 95 offer handy hints for selecting the right plants. "Gardens for Sun" on page 96 and "Gardens for Shade" on page 97 discuss the factors you'll need to consider on these sites. "Basic Care for Flowers" on page 98 covers the information you need to plant and care for a healthy garden. For information on specific flowers, see "Low-maintenance Flowers," starting on page 100.

Opposite: For easy-care color all season long, fill your flower beds with a variety of annuals. Many annuals, including cornflowers (*Centaurea cyanus*), will self-sow for an informal, cottage-garden look.

Designing a Low-maintenance Flower Garden

Creating a low-maintenance flower garden begins the same way designing any landscape feature does—with a plan, however scribbled or sketchy. There are two ways to approach this process. You can figure out where you want the garden to go, then pick from the group of low-maintenance flowers that are adapted to the growing conditions available. Or if you know what flowers you really want to grow, you can plan a garden that will provide the conditions those flowers need. Either way, matching the plants and the site is a key part of making a low-maintenance flower garden.

Picking the Site

Maybe you already know right where you want your new flower garden to be. Or perhaps you know which flowers you want to grow, and you've found a spot on

Large flower beds are beautiful but hard to maintain. Make beds narrow enough so you can reach plants in the middle.

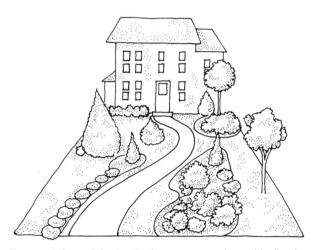

For an informal look, design your garden with flowing curves and a variety of planting areas.

Straight lines and symmetrical plantings will give your garden a much more formal appearance.

If you like the casual look of a cottage garden, sow a mixture of plants that are adapted to your conditions.

your property that offers the right growing conditions. Now it's time to sketch out a rough plan.

First think about the shape and size of your beds. Do you want the straight lines of a formal garden or the curving outlines of an informal one? Try laying out a rope to get a better idea of how possible bed outlines will look. Make the bed narrow enough so you can easily reach plants when you want to pinch off a dead flower or check a leaf for insects. If you'll only have access from one side, make the bed equal to (or slightly less than) the distance you can reach comfortably. If you'll be able to tend the plants from both sides, the bed can be twice the width of your reach.

Scrutinize your plan to see if it will create maintenance headaches and how they can be avoided. Are the beds under the gutterless edge of a roof? If so, plant beyond the water drop-off line, and prevent splashing soil with a row of flagstones or a strip of large gravel.

Is the bed adjacent to lawn? Keep the grass out with a strip of bricks or some other easy-care edging (see "End Edging Forever" on page 43 for tips on installing mowing strips). If you see potential problems that you can't avoid, like seedlings from overhanging trees, consider moving or adjusting the size of the bed. Or be prepared to do a little more maintenance for the sake of having your flower bed right where you want it.

Choosing the Plants

For most people, deciding which flowers to grow is the most fun part of the process. If you simply must have certain plants, like pansies or peonies, you'll need to find a spot in your yard that provides the right growing conditions. Rethink your plant choices seriously if you can't provide the right growing conditions. No matter how much you want phlox or bee balm, for example, that large shade tree in your backyard will block the sun those plants need to thrive. Yes, sun-loving plants may live in shade, but they won't grow and flower well, and they'll be much more prone to pests and diseases (leading to more maintenance).

You can grow almost any flower in an open sunny area, especially if the soil is well drained. If you plant along the west or south side of a house or fence, you'll need flowers that can take the reflected heat and light. If you're planting in the shade, your choices are limited to flowering and foliage plants that require little light. When you choose plants, you'll want to group the ones with similar needs in the beds that best meet those needs.

Prepare a rough list of the plants you want to put into the garden. Then start thinking about how you could arrange those plants to make them look good together. Below are some handy tips to keep in mind as you plan the design.

Exercise Restraint Mass plantings of one kind of plant, or a combination of big groups of three or four types, are more effective than sprinklings of a few plants of a dozen different species.

Plan for Season-long Bloom To have something flowering most of the season, include plants that bloom early, late, and in between. For early spring color, bulbs like daffodils are easy. Annuals provide dependable color during the summer and hide the browning leaves of early perennials. For the fall, consider late bloomers like chrysanthemums and Japanese anemone (*Anemone* x *hybrida*).

Combine Colors You Like Don't let rigid design rules limit your creativity. With today's less formal gardening styles, you can plant whatever looks good to you. Some gardeners like to balance colors by using lots of white flowers throughout the planting. Gray and pale yellow flowers are also helpful for blending different colors.

Another good approach, especially for small plantings, is to use different colors of the same plant. The consistency of height and texture balances the variations in color. And it makes it easier to take care of the planting, since all the plants have the same light, water, and soil requirements.

Balance the Heights If you're planting a border along a fence or the house, set the tallest plants in the back, the medium ones in the middle, and the short ones in front. (For easier maintenance, leave a small path between the structure and the back row of plants.) If you're planting a bed that you can reach from all sides (called an island bed), the tall plants go in the center, the short ones go on the outside, and the medium ones go in between. To keep the garden from looking too rigid, though, bring some midsized plants to the front here and there. And overlap the plants where different heights meet.

Bulbs and flowering shrubs offer bright color for a minimum of maintenance. Daffodils with early rhododendrons are one of the possible easy-care combinations you can create.

Easy Annuals

Annual flowers are great for low-maintenance gardens. They're easy to grow, as long as they get the light and water they need. They come in just about every color and height you'd want. They're inexpensive, so you get a big effect for a little money; and if one isn't healthy, you can toss it out without much anguish. In addition, you can plant most annuals as late as early summer, if you don't get around to spring gardening as soon as you'd like.

Below you'll find information on buying and starting annuals for your garden. For details on soil preparation, planting, and aftercare, see "Basic Care for Flowers" on page 98.

Starting from Seed

You can grow your annuals from seed or buy transplants. Growing them from seed is less expensive and gives you a greater choice of cultivars. But you have to sow most annuals indoors 6 weeks before you move them outside, which means you have to worry about soil mixes, moisture, temperature, light, and all the other factors that influence success with seeds. Starting your own annuals indoors from seed can be fun and rewarding, but it's not the route to go if you really want minimal maintenance. Fortunately, many colorful, low-care annuals—including marigolds and zinnias—are easy to start by sowing seeds directly where you want them to grow. Follow the information on the seed packets for sowing times and depths.

Starting with Transplants

Buying transplants is much easier than starting seeds indoors, and it is still relatively inexpensive. Just figure

California poppy is an easy-to-grow annual for sunny gardens: Just scatter the seed in a well-drained spot.

out how many plants you need and head to the garden center around planting time. (For most annuals, this is around the average date of the last frost for your area. If you're not sure of your last frost date, ask your gardening neighbors or the local Cooperative Extension Service.)

As you pick through the stock, try to avoid buying plants that are already blooming—they'll take longer to make new roots. Put back any that have discolored stems or leaves, holes in the leaves, or any other sign of disease or insect damage. Don't buy annuals that are spindly or pale; look for compact, leafy, deep green plants. When possible, set transplants out on a cloudy day, so they'll be less prone to transplant shock.

If you don't want to bother with seeds, start with compact, healthy-looking transplants from a local garden center.

Easy Annuals from Seed

Save the step of transplanting by sowing seeds of these tough annuals directly in the garden.

Calendula officinalis (pot marigold)
Centaurea cyanus (cornflower)
Clarkia amoena (farewell-to-spring)
Cleome hasslerana (spider flower)
Consolida ambigua (rocket larkspur)
Eschscholzia californica (California poppy)
Helianthus annuus (common sunflower)
Lathyrus odoratus (sweet pea)
Lobularia maritima (sweet alyssum)
Nigella damascena (love-in-a-mist)
Papaver rhoeas (corn poppy)
Portulaca grandiflora (rose moss)
Tagetes spp. (marigolds)

Low-maintenance Perennials and Bulbs

Adding perennials to a low-maintenance landscape requires some thought. Compared to most annuals, perennials flower for a shorter period, so you have to figure out what will be blooming when and whether it will look good with its neighbors. They're more expensive, so you'll want to provide them with ideal conditions to keep them healthy and vigorous. And you have to plant early—sometimes the preceding fall—to get good color this season.

Why take the trouble? Because well-chosen perennials, once established, come back year after year with little or no help from you. Some give color in the early spring, just when your late-winter depression verges on true dementia. Their successive bloom seasons give you an incentive to get outside and walk around the yard to see what's flowering. For some, perennials bring back fond memories of favorite people or places from the past.

Below are some tips for choosing perennials for your yard. "Basic Care for Flowers" on page 98 gives the details on planting and maintaining your flowers.

Picking Easy-care Perennials

If you really want to avoid labor, shun tall or floppy plants—like hybrid delphinium (*Delphinium* x *elatum*) and baby's-breath (*Gypsophila paniculata*)—that need staking. Steer clear of tender perennials, such as canna (*Canna* x *generalis*) and dahlia (*Dahlia* spp.), that you have to dig up and store over the winter. Unless you want to cover a large area, avoid those that spread, like lamb's-ears (*Stachys byzantina*) and goutweed (*Aegopodium podagraria*). Pass up those that die out after a few years, like many perennial asters (*Aster* spp.). And don't plant those that have a serious pest in your area, unless you can get a resistant cultivar.

What's left? A lot, starting with dependable spring bulbs like crocuses and daffodils; irises, if iris borer isn't a severe problem in your area; daylilies (there are thousands to choose from); and hostas, for shady areas.

After a long, dreary winter, what could be more welcome that a cheerful planting of dependable, easy-care crocus?

Try short cultivars of balloon flower (*Platycodon grandiflorus*) and bellflowers (*Campanula* spp.). Choose coreopsis (*Corepsis* spp.) and other native wildflowers, especially in a natural garden. Don't forget old-time favorites like bleeding heart (*Dicentra* spp.). Ornamental grasses like fountain grass (*Pennisetum alopecuroides*) and blue fescue (*Festuca cinerea*) are great for their foliage and interesting seed heads.

The list goes on. For more ideas, look at gardens that bloom even though you know no one bothers with them. Before you plant any perennial, research its growth requirements to be sure it suits your conditions. "Low-maintenance Flowers," starting on page 100, covers growing information for many easy-care flowers.

Perennial balloon flower produces inflated, balloon-like buds that open to saucer-shaped blue-purple flowers. To avoid staking, look for short selections like the cultivar 'Apoyama'.

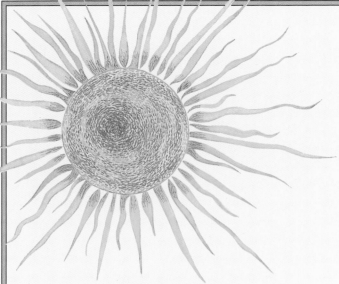

Gardens for Sun

You'll spend the least time tinkering with your sunny garden if you choose plants that can take the heat. Consider the wide variety of fabulous flowers that thrive in full sun and can withstand dry spells.

Of course, during a drought, even tough plants might need watering. A soaker hose is a great watering tool for flower beds or any place plants are close together because water seeps out gently along the length of the hose. There are two types of soaker hoses. The first, sometimes called a leaky pipe, is made of a rough black rubbery material that's covered with tiny pores that ooze water. The other type has holes in a band that runs the length of the hose. If you turn the band of holes

Make watering your sunny garden a snap by adding soaker hoses; they'll ooze water into the soil for thirsty roots.

face up, they work like mini-sprinklers. Turn it down (the ideal placement) and you soak the soil. Connect either type directly to an outdoor faucet or to the end of a regular garden hose if you don't want to water the stretch of land between the faucet and the garden. For the ultimate convenience, you can attach a timer to the hose to turn it on and off automatically.

You'll water and weed less if you surround the plants with a layer of organic mulch 1 to 3 inches (2.5 to 7.5 cm) thick. Apply the mulch after your direct-sown seedlings are about 6 inches (15 cm) tall and you've put in your transplants.

Sun-loving Plants

The secret to an easy-care garden in the sun is to pick plants that need lots of light and aren't fussy about their soil. It's even easier if they also don't need much water (like the perennials listed below). Here are a few of the best easy-care annuals and perennials for sun:

Annuals
Ageratum houstonianum (ageratum)
Antirrhinum majus (common snapdragon)
Calendula officinalis (pot marigold)
Centaurea cyanus (cornflower)
Helianthus annuus (common sunflower)
Lobularia maritima (sweet alyssum)
Nicotiana alata (flowering tobacco)
Verbena x *hybrida* (garden verbena)
Zinnia elegans (common zinnia)
Perennials
Armeria maritima (thrift)
Coreopsis spp. (coreopsis)
Echinacea purpurea (purple coneflower)
Hemerocallis spp. (daylily)
Rudbeckia spp. (coneflowers)
Sedum spectabile (showy stonecrop)

Zinnias are colorful and easy to grow, but tall cultivars will need staking. Choose compact cultivars for less work.

Gardens for Shade

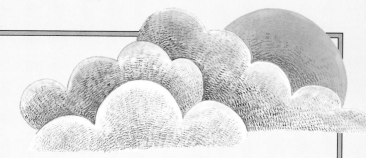

Don't despair if you have shade! Your garden may not overflow with great masses of color, but you can still enjoy the beautiful annuals and perennials that prefer less sunshine.

As you plan your shade garden, don't forget to consider the many plants with beautiful foliage. Besides providing a good background for surrounding flowers, plants with attractive leaves can themselves provide season-long interest. Along with all the varying shades of green, leaves come in many colors, including silvery blue, blue-green, yellow-green, and purple. Plants with multicolored (variegated) leaves are also good choices for adding sparkle to a shady corner. Hostas are available in many leaf colors and variegations, and they flower as well. Several species of lungworts (*Pulmonaria* spp.) offer silver-speckled leaves, along with pink-and-blue spring flowers. Coleus, ferns, hellebores (*Helleborus* spp.), and lamiums (*Lamium* spp.) are other natural choices for foliage interest. If you're gardening under shallow-rooted trees like maples and beeches, look for drought-tolerant shade-lovers like barrenworts (*Epimedium* spp.) and yellow archangel (*Lamiastrum galeobdolon* 'Herman's Pride').

Shade gardens need less water because the drying sun doesn't beat down on them. But they also are perfect for fungal diseases that like humid, cool, dark conditions. For that reason, it's important to space shade plants at the distance recommended—or even wider—to get good air movement. When you do water, irrigate so you wet the soil rather than the leaves.

Slugs, being fond of moist areas, can be troublesome in shade gardens. If you're finding holes in your leaves (hostas are a favorite target), encircle the bed with a strip of copper edging to keep the pests out. (Catch slugs that are already inside the bed by trapping them in fruit rinds set upside down on the soil surface; check traps and remove pests daily until the problem decreases.)

Low-care Shade-loving Plants

If your site gets some direct sun for part of the day, or light shade all day, you can still grow a variety of annuals and perennials. A few of the best are listed below:

Annuals
Begonia Semperflorens-Cultorum hybrid (wax begonia)
Celosia cristata (cockscomb)
Impatiens wallerana (impatiens)
Lobelia erinus (edging lobelia)
Nicotiana alata (flowering tobacco)

Perennials
Aquilegia spp. (columbines)
Astilbe spp. (astilbes)
Cimicifuga spp. (bugbanes)
Dicentra spp. (bleeding hearts)
Hosta spp. (hostas)
Pulmonaria spp. (lungworts)

Add season-long interest to a shady area with beautiful foliage and flowering plants. For a moist spot, try a combination of blue-leaved hostas, colorful primroses, and spiky irises.

Basic Care for Flowers

With just a little routine care, your gardens can be filled with flowers all season long. Preparing the soil well is critical for getting plants off to a good start. Mulching is another important step, since it adds nutrients, reduces watering, and cuts down on weeding. Other steps, like grooming and dividing, can be done when you have a few moments to spare.

Soil Preparation

Whether you're planting annuals or perennials, make sure the flower bed is ready when they arrive. To prepare a new annual bed, turn the soil with a spade, working in compost or another fine-textured organic material. In following years, just add organic matter and turn the soil lightly with a spading fork before planting. Perennials have deeper roots and stay in place longer, so they appreciate more thorough soil preparation. If you can, invest some time and effort into double-digging your perennial beds. Once it's done, you don't have to do it again; just set in your perennials and watch them thrive.

Planting

Setting annual transplants or container-grown perennials into prepared soil is easy. Support the crown of each plant on one hand as you invert the pot with the other hand. Slide the plant out of the pot without pulling on the stem. (Give the base of the container a few hard taps on a solid surface if the plant won't come out.) If you see any roots circling the exposed soil ball, try to free them gently with your fingers. If the roots

Mulching is a key part of a low-maintenance flower garden. It keeps weeds down and helps the soil stay moist.

are tightly matted, loosen them by using a knife to make four shallow cuts on the outside of the root mass.

Dig a hole large enough to hold the whole root ball comfortably. Set the plant in the center of the hole, so it is sitting at the same level that it grew at in the container. Fill in around the roots with soil, and water the plant well to settle it in.

Watering

Most flowering plants let you know it's time to water by wilting, especially when the sun is hottest. But for best growth, try to keep the ground evenly moist. If it hasn't rained for a week or so, pull back the mulch and dig a hole about 3 inches (7.5 cm) deep. If the soil at that level is moist, wait a day or two and check again.

You'll save water by putting it directly on the soil rather than by watering over the top with a sprinkler. A soaker hose works well in flower beds because water seeps out the length of it. For more details on using soaker hoses, see "Gardens for Sun" on page 96.

Fertilizing and Mulching

If you've prepared the soil well, your plants should grow fine with just an

Easy-care plants like rose moss (*Portulaca grandiflora*) give you loads of color for minimal work. They'll thrive even without regular watering, mulching, or fertilizing.

organic mulch. Apply a 1-inch (2.5 cm) layer of compost, grass clippings, or other fine-textured organic material after seedlings are several inches tall and the transplants are in. To suppress weeds, top the fine mulch with a 2-inch layer of bark mulch. It will be easy to pull any weeds that pop through the mulch.

If you have time and inclination, you can get more blooms by fertilizing with liquid seaweed every month or so. Spray it on the leaves, or drench the soil around the plant with it. To help perennials through cold winters, apply a deep winter mulch after the ground has frozen. Use leaves, pine boughs, straw, or another loose material. Remove mulch in early spring.

Grooming

To encourage bushiness in annuals, you can pinch off the growing point at the very top of the plants when they're about 6 inches (15 cm) tall. Deadheading—removing spent flowers—can encourage many plants to bloom longer, but it's not necessary, especially if you want low-maintenance plantings.

Dividing

For the ultimate low-maintenance perennial garden, you would only have slow-growing perennials like peonies, baptisias (*Baptisia* spp.), and torch lilies (*Kniphofia* spp.), which seldom, if ever, need division. But there are many other dependable, easy-to-grow perennials that will thrive in your garden if you're willing to divide them every few years.

It's time to divide when a clump flowers poorly or its center dies out. The best time to divide is usually in early spring; second choice is the late fall before the ground freezes. For shallow-rooted plants, like asters and chrysanthemums, dig up the clump and separate the baby plants by hand, leaving a few healthy shoots on each section. For plants that multiply by sending out creeping stems (like bee balms, *Monarda* spp.), just cut the runners and dig up the baby plants, soil and all. For deep-rooted clumps—such as daylilies and ornamental grasses—either slice off a chunk with a spade or dig the whole thing up and pry sections off by hand or with a spading fork. Replant some of the divisions into enriched soil and share extras with friends.

Plant spring bulbs with bushy perennials that can hide the ripening foliage and fill in when bulbs go dormant.

Achillea filipendulina   Compositae

FERN-LEAVED YARROW

The showy flower heads of fern-leaved yarrow add an abundance of color to the summer garden. Plant it where the soil tends to be dry; otherwise, the stems may need staking.

TYPE OF PLANT: Perennial.

SEASON OF INTEREST: Gold flowers, carried in flat, umbrella-like clusters, rise over feathery leaves in summer.

BEST CLIMATE AND SITE: Zones 3–9. Thrives in full sun and well-drained soil of average fertility. Tolerates drought.

GROWING GUIDELINES: Limit fertilizer so the plant grows slowly and stays compact and self-supporting. Remove old flowers, cutting the stem back to new buds or to the base. Divide every 3 years to renew the clump.

PEST AND DISEASE PREVENTION: Plants are generally problem-free.

LANDSCAPE USE: Height of flower stalks to 4 feet (1.2 m). The foliage remains quite low but can spread on creeping roots to a width of 3 feet (90 cm). Yarrows are excellent for the flower garden. For sharp contrast, combine with cool-colored flowers like blue sages (*Salvia* spp.).

RELATED PLANTS:

COMMON YARROW (*A. millefolium*): Has red, pink, or white flowers.

WOOLY YARROW (*A. tomentosa*): Low-growing; has silver leaves and gold flowers on 12-inch (30 cm) stalks.

Alchemilla mollis   Rosaceae

LADY'S-MANTLE

Lovely lady's-mantle produces frothy sprays of greenish yellow flowers in summer. If the foliage starts to look tattered, cut it down for a new flush of leaves.

TYPE OF PLANT: Perennial.

SEASON OF INTEREST: Sprays of tiny, greenish yellow flowers in summer are good for cutting. Delicate, furry, scalloped leaves are attractive throughout the growing season.

BEST CLIMATE AND SITE: Zones 4–8. Full sun; light shade in hot climates; evenly moist, but not soggy, soil.

GROWING GUIDELINES: Water during drought to prevent leaf browning. Deadhead after flowering or leave a few flowers on so the plant can self-sow. If the foliage begins to look shabby, cut the stems back by about a third. Divide in early spring or fall if you want more plants.

PEST AND DISEASE PREVENTION: Apply water at ground level during hot, humid weather to keep leaves dry and discourage fungal diseases.

LANDSCAPE USE: Height to 12 inches (30 cm); slightly broader spread. Use to edge the front of a shrub or flower bed or mass it into a groundcover. Set clumps in front of tall plants with barren lower stems, like old fashioned shrub roses. Or set beside bright flowers like annual red sage to soften their vivid color.

RELATED PLANTS:

ALPINE LADY'S-MANTLE (*A. alpina*): Forms a tidy clump to 8 inches (20 cm) tall; has divided leaves edged with white. Zones 3–7.

Amsonia tabernaemontana   Apocynaceae

WILLOW BLUE STAR

Depend on willow blue star for season-long interest. It has clusters of blue flowers in late spring, bushy clumps of willow-like leaves in summer, and yellow fall color.

TYPE OF PLANT: Perennial.

SEASON OF INTEREST: Delicate clusters of pastel blue flowers in late spring or early summer. In fall, the lanky willow-like leaves turn gold before the plant dies back.

BEST CLIMATE AND SITE: Zones 3–9. Light shade; moist soil. In Northern climates, may also tolerate full sun.

GROWING GUIDELINES: Water in drought. If the plant gets too tall in shady locations, pinch the young shoot tips.

PEST AND DISEASE PREVENTION: Plants are generally problem-free.

LANDSCAPE USE: Height to 3 feet (90 cm). Set clumps along the edge of woods or tree groves. Use beside a stream or pond or in a flower border. When flowering, blue star looks good with low-growing violets or pansies. When showing fall color, it contrasts beautifully with purple fall asters.

OTHER COMMENTS: *A. tabernaemontana* var. *montana* stays 15 inches (37.5 cm) high.

Anemone x _hybrida_   Ranunculaceae

JAPANESE ANEMONE

Add late color to a shady garden with the beautiful flowers of Japanese anemones. Long-stemmed cultivars may sprawl in windy areas; choose compact selections to avoid staking.

TYPE OF PLANT: Perennial.

SEASON OF INTEREST: Long-stemmed masses of pink, white, or red flowers in fall. They are a welcome change from the traditional gold, orange, and bronze colors of the season. The dark green, divided leaves add subtle charm through the spring and summer.

BEST CLIMATE AND SITE: Zones 5–8. Prefers a few hours of afternoon shade; moist, well-drained soil. Shelter from winds.

GROWING GUIDELINES: Shoots are slow to emerge in spring. Mark their location so you do not dig among them by mistake. Water during dry or hot weather.

PEST AND DISEASE PREVENTION: Plant in well-drained soil to avoid root rot.

LANDSCAPE USE: Height 3–5 feet (90–120 cm). Spectacular if you let it spread in large groups in a flower border or bright woodland edge. You can also put it in flower or shrub borders or in a cut-flower garden.

OTHER COMMENTS: To avoid staking, plant compact cultivars such as 'Kriemhilde' or 'Pamina'.

RELATED PLANTS:

GRAPE-LEAVED ANEMONE (_A. vitifolia_): Single pink or white flowers in late summer. Can spread vigorously.

Armeria maritima   Plumbaginaceae

COMMON THRIFT

Plant the grassy evergreen clumps of common thrift as a tidy edging for shrub or flower borders. Pink flowers atop wiry stems bloom above the clumps in early summer.

TYPE OF PLANT: Perennial.

SEASON OF INTEREST: Wiry stems are topped with 1-inch (2.5 cm) balls of flowers in early summer and occasionally afterward. Throughout the rest of the year, you'll enjoy the neat clump of low grass-like foliage.

BEST CLIMATE AND SITE: Zones 4–8. Sun; well-drained soil. Seems to thrive on neglect, enjoying sandy sites sprayed with salty sea air.

GROWING GUIDELINES: Don't fertilize; rich soil causes plants to die out in the center. Remove the flowering stalk at the base after the flower fades to encourage reblooming.

PEST AND DISEASE PREVENTION: If you plant in well-drained soil of low fertility, this plant generally is problem-free.

LANDSCAPE USE: Height to 12 inches (30 cm) when flowering. Use as tidy edge for the front of a flower or shrub bed or in a rock garden. Goes well with blue-flowered ajugas (_Ajuga_ spp.).

RELATED PLANTS:

A. juniperifolia: Denser foliage and pink flowers that only reach 6 inches (15 cm) high.

A. pseudarmeria: Wider leaves and white to pink flowers; grows to 15 inches (37.5 cm) high.

WHITE MUGWORT

White mugwort bears showy plumes of fragrant white flowers in late summer. Unlike its silver-leaved relatives, white mugwort needs moist soil and can take light shade.

TYPE OF PLANT: Perennial.

SEASON OF INTEREST: A spectacular show of graceful, 2-foot (60 cm) long plumes of fragrant white flowers in late summer. The rest of the season you'll enjoy the deeply cut bright green foliage.

BEST CLIMATE AND SITE: Zones 5–8. Does best in full sun but will tolerate light shade; moist, fertile soil.

GROWING GUIDELINES: Fertilize lightly in spring. Water during drought.

PEST AND DISEASE PREVENTION: Plants are generally problem-free.

LANDSCAPE USE: Height 4–6 feet (1.2–1.8 m); width to 4 feet (1.2 m). Give plenty of space. Makes a nice background plant in a flower border, especially when highlighted by lower-growing coneflowers (*Rudbeckia* spp.), daylilies, or asters.

RELATED PLANTS: Many species of *Artemisia* have silver foliage and require full sun and dry soil. They include the following:

A. x 'Powis Castle' has finely cut leaves on stems up to 36 inches (90 cm); no flowers.

A. schmidtiana 'Silver Mound' grows into a neat mound of silver foliage 12 inches (30 cm) high.

NEW YORK ASTER

Late-blooming New York aster is a colorful addition to the fall garden. Divide clumps every year or two to keep them vigorous; pinch in early summer to promote strong stems.

TYPE OF PLANT: Perennial.

SEASON OF INTEREST: Blazes with white, blue, purple, or pink flowers in late summer and early fall.

BEST CLIMATE AND SITE: Zones 3–8. Sun; moist, well-drained soil of moderate fertility.

GROWING GUIDELINES: Pinch asters once or twice before June 15 to make them bushier and less likely to need staking. Divide every 1–2 years to renew the plant. Mulch during winter in Zone 4.

PEST AND DISEASE PREVENTION: Don't overcrowd; needs plenty of fresh air to avoid mildew.

LANDSCAPE USE: Height 1–6 feet (30–180 cm), depending on the cultivar. Use in clumps or masses in flower or mixed borders. Asters look good with chrysanthemums and goldenrods (*Solidago* spp.).

RELATED PLANTS: There are scores of good aster species including:

FRIKART'S ASTER (*A.* x *frikartii*): Long-blooming; lavender-blue flowers from midsummer into fall.

HEATH ASTER (*A. ericoides*): Durable American native; profusion of small white flowers in late summer.

NEW ENGLAND ASTER (*A. novae-angliae*): Tends to be tall and flower in pink, red, lavender, and violet. More resistant to mildew than the New York asters.

Astilbe x *arendsii*   Saxifragaceae

ASTILBE

Astilbes are longtime favorites for spring and summer bloom in moist, shady spots. Remove the flowers when they fade, or leave them on the plant for winter interest.

TYPE OF PLANT: Perennial.

SEASON OF INTEREST: White, pink, or red feathery flower plumes in late spring and early summer. Throughout the rest of the growing season you'll enjoy the divided, deep green, glossy leaves.

BEST CLIMATE AND SITE: Zones 4–9. Grows best in light to medium shade but may be able to tolerate more sun as long as the soil is moist enough. Rich, moist—even wet—soil.

GROWING GUIDELINES: Add extra organic matter to the bed before planting. Water if the soil begins to dry out to keep the leaves from browning around the edges. Mulch with compost. Fertilize with a balanced organic fertilizer in early spring. You can remove the faded flowers or leave them on for winter interest.

PEST AND DISEASE PREVENTION: Plants are generally problem-free.

LANDSCAPE USE: Height 2–4 feet (60–120 cm); width 2–3 feet (30–60 cm), depending on the cultivar. Create a spectacular mass near a stream, pond, or woodland edge. For a smaller shade garden, plant each cultivar in clumps of three.

RELATED PLANTS:

CHINESE ASTILBE (*A. chinensis*): Height to 3 feet (90 cm); rose, lavender, or purple flowers.

STAR ASTILBE (*A. simplicifolia*): Height to 12 inches (30 cm); spikes of pink, white, or rose flowers.

Baptisia australis   Leguminosae

BLUE FALSE INDIGO

Blue false indigo forms shrub-like clumps of blue-green leaves topped with spikes of blue flowers in late spring. Plants may need staking in shade or moist soil.

TYPE OF PLANT: Perennial.

SEASON OF INTEREST: Flashy 1-foot (30 cm) spikes of vibrant blue flowers in late spring. The flowers can last as long as a month, then they turn into handsome seedpods. The bluish leaves resemble clover.

BEST CLIMATE AND SITE: Zones 3–9. Full sun; well-drained soil. You may have to stake the plant if you grow it in fertile, moist soil or light shade. Tolerates drought.

GROWING GUIDELINES: Deadhead to extend the flowering period. Seldom needs division.

PEST AND DISEASE PREVENTION: Plants are generally problem-free.

LANDSCAPE USE: Height and width to 4 feet (1.2 m). Ideal massed in the back of a flower garden. Use a single specimen in the middle of the border to frame the view behind. Try blending it with yellow irises or mixing it into a meadow garden.

RELATED PLANTS:

WHITE WILD INDIGO (*B. alba*): Height to 3 feet (90 cm); bears white flowers.

YELLOW WILD INDIGO (*B. tinctora*): Height to 4 feet (1.2 m); bears yellow flowers.

Boltonia asteroides   Compositae

BOLTONIA

Easy-to-grow boltonia produces masses of white, daisy-like blooms in late summer and fall. Pinch the stems in early summer to promote sturdier, more compact growth.

TYPE OF PLANT: Perennial.

SEASON OF INTEREST: Erupts with clouds of white or pink daisy-like flowers in late summer and fall.

BEST CLIMATE AND SITE: Zones 3–9. Grows best in full sun; in light shade, you'll probably have to stake it. Plant in well-drained soil enriched with organic matter.

GROWING GUIDELINES: To avoid staking, look for compact cultivars such as 'Snowbank'. Water during drought.

PEST AND DISEASE PREVENTION: Plants are generally problem-free.

LANDSCAPE USE: Height 5–6 feet (1.5–1.8 m); width 4 feet (1.2 m). Give it lots of room at the back of the border. Set lower plants by its feet to hide the sometimes barren lower stem. For contrast, blend pink-flowered cultivar 'Pink Beauty' with Russian sage (*Perovskia atriplicifolia*) or white boltonia with goldenrods (*Solidago* spp.).

Campanula carpatica   Campanulaceae

CARPATHIAN HAREBELL

Adaptable Carpathian harebell spreads to form tidy mounds of dark green leaves topped with cup-shaped, blue-purple flowers. Mulch to keep the roots cool in warm climates.

TYPE OF PLANT: Perennial.

SEASON OF INTEREST: Lively blue-purple or white flowers in early summer.

BEST CLIMATE AND SITE: Zones 3–8. Full sun; light shade in hotter sites; well-drained, moist, fertile soil.

GROWING GUIDELINES: Short-lived unless you divide and renew every couple of years. Mulch with compost during summer. Water in drought. Deadhead for an extended bloom period or leave a few flowers on so the plant can self-sow.

PEST AND DISEASE PREVENTION: Trap slugs and snails in saucers of beer set shallowly in the ground near the plants.

LANDSCAPE USE: Height to 9 inches (22.5 cm); slightly wider spread. Set in clumps or rows in front of a flower or shrub border. Or use plants individually in a rock garden or beside a stone patio.

RELATED PLANTS:

CANTERBURY BELLS (*C. medium*): Biennial; produces 3-foot (90 cm) tall spikes of large pink, white, or blue flowers in early summer.

CLUSTERED BELLFLOWER (*C. glomerata*): Bears thick clusters of blue flowers in early summer. It can spread aggressively.

PEACH-LEAVED BELLFLOWER (*C. persicifolia*): Has blue or white flowers on 3-foot (90 cm) stems in summer.

Catharanthus roseus   Apocynaceae

MADAGASCAR PERIWINKLE

Heat-loving Madagascar periwinkle grows easily from transplants and blooms from spring through frost. Try it in flower borders, window boxes, or hanging baskets.

TYPE OF PLANT: Commonly grown as an annual, though it can be perennial in frost-free climates.

SEASON OF INTEREST: White, pink, or rose flowers throughout the frost-free growing season.

BEST CLIMATE AND SITE: All Zones. Full sun; well-drained soil. Will tolerate drought but grows best in lightly moist soil.

GROWING GUIDELINES: Buy nursery-grown plants; Madagascar periwinkle grows slowly from seed. Plant self-branching cultivars such as 'Pretty in White' and 'Pretty in Rose' to avoid pinching lanky plants.

PEST AND DISEASE PREVENTION: Plants are generally problem-free.

LANDSCAPE USE: Height and spread to 1 foot (30 cm). Use with other annuals; it looks good with blue ageratums. Edge a garden with it or let it dangle over the rim of a hanging basket or window box.

Cleome hasslerana   Caparaceae

CLEOME

Clumps of tall annual cleome can add a dramatic touch to any garden. These plants often self-sow, and their seedlings pop up in the most surprising places!

TYPE OF PLANT: Annual.

SEASON OF INTEREST: Clusters of pink, purple, or white flowers with long spidery stamens in summer and fall. Flowers stand above bold, palmately cut, sticky leaves.

BEST CLIMATE AND SITE: All Zones. Grows best in full sun but will tolerate light shade. Thrives in heat if you give it moist, well-drained soil.

GROWING GUIDELINES: Grows easily from seed sown indoors 4 weeks before the last frost. Plants may also self-sow. If desired, pinch long stems to encourage more compact growth. Water during drought.

PEST AND DISEASE PREVENTION: Plants are generally problem-free.

LANDSCAPE USE: Height to 4 feet (1.2 m). Use in a large annual bed; looks good in front of large-leaved castor beans (*Ricinus communis*) or behind blue-flowered sages (*Salvia* spp.) and 'Purple Ruffles' basil.

Colchicum autumnale Liliaceae

FALL CROCUS

Showy fall crocus will surprise you by popping their flowers out of the ground in fall. The strap-like leaves don't appear until spring. Plant dormant bulbs in midsummer.

TYPE OF PLANT: Bulb.

SEASON OF INTEREST: Clusters of low-growing lavender, pink, or white flowers emerge without leaves in fall. (Long broad leaves emerge in spring and go dormant by midsummer.)

BEST CLIMATE AND SITE: Zones 4–9. Sun or, at most, a couple hours of shade; well-drained, moist soil.

GROWING GUIDELINES: Mulch the growing plant with compost in spring. Remove the foliage when it yellows in summer and mark the dormant plant's location so you won't damage it.

PEST AND DISEASE PREVENTION: Plants are generally problem-free.

LANDSCAPE USE: Think carefully about where to grow this plant. It has wide leaves that grow to a height of 15 inches (37.5 cm) and can look awkward in nooks and crannies that are ideal for the low fall flowers. Try it amid shrubs, rocks, groundcovers, or low-growing annuals.

OTHER COMMENTS: Fall crocus is poisonous.

RELATED PLANTS:

SHOWY CROCUS (*C. speciosus*): Produces a larger leafy clump in spring and white, red, purple, or lavender flowers in fall.

Coreopsis verticillata Compositae

THREAD-LEAVED COREOPSIS

Thread-leaved coreopsis is a great choice for sure-fire summer color. Give them a well-drained site with full sun; the stems tend to flop in moist or rich soil.

TYPE OF PLANT: Perennial.

SEASON OF INTEREST: Dainty yellow flowers for most of the summer and into fall. Arching branches of feathery foliage form a graceful mound.

BEST CLIMATE AND SITE: Zones 3–9. Full sun; well-drained soil.

GROWING GUIDELINES: Trim back the ends of the stems after the first flush of bloom to encourage reblooming. You also can cut them back more severely, by about half, if the plant starts to flop. Divide after several years to renew. Tolerates drought.

PEST AND DISEASE PREVENTION: Plants are generally problem-free.

LANDSCAPE USE: Height 18–36 inches (45–90 cm); similar spread. Use alone or in masses. For contrast, blend it with purple-colored sages (*Salvia* spp.) and 'Autumn Joy' sedum (*Sedum* 'Autumn Joy'). Or use near spring-flowering bulbs to hide the fading foliage.

RELATED PLANTS:

LANCE-LEAVED COREOPSIS (*C. lanceolata*): Has broader, divided leaves and larger, gold flowers.

PINK TICKSEED (*C. rosea*): Has pink flowers and similar feathery foliage.

| *Cosmos bipinnatus* | Compositae | *Crocus* hybrids | Iridaceae |

COSMOS

CROCUS

Cosmos is loved by many gardeners for its large, bright flowers that bloom from summer through fall. The cultivar 'Seashells', with rolled petals, is particularly elegant.

Early-blooming crocus are a welcome sight in the spring garden. Combine them with low-growing groundcovers or annuals that can hide the ripening bulb foliage.

TYPE OF PLANT: Annual.

SEASON OF INTEREST: Airy sprays of pink, red, and white flowers from midsummer into fall. They stand over upright stems clothed in ferny foliage.

BEST CLIMATE AND SITE: All Zones. Full sun; well-drained soil, preferably of below-average fertility.

GROWING GUIDELINES: Sprinkle seed on a prepared garden bed after the last spring frost. Thin seedlings to the spacing recommended on the seed packet. Remove the old flowers when they fade or leave a few to self-sow.

PEST AND DISEASE PREVENTION: Plants are generally problem-free.

LANDSCAPE USE: Height 2–4 feet (60–120 cm), depending on the cultivar. You can let it naturalize in a sunny flower garden, work it into vacant spots in a perennial border, or confine it to a cut-flower garden.

RELATED PLANTS:

YELLOW COSMOS (*C. sulphureus*): Height to 2 feet (60 cm). Bears yellow and orange flowers above marigold-like foliage.

TYPE OF PLANT: Bulb.

SEASON OF INTEREST: Crocus are among the first bulbs to welcome spring, scattering purple, white, and yellow flowers across early spring landscapes. The leaves, which look like grass with a white stripe down the center, die back in early summer.

BEST CLIMATE AND SITE: Zones 3–8. Sun or light shade; well-drained soil enriched with organic matter.

GROWING GUIDELINES: Plant bulbs in fall. Deadhead after blooming. Cut the foliage off only after it has yellowed.

PEST AND DISEASE PREVENTION: Protect from bulb-eating rodents by planting groups in a sunken wire mesh cage. Plant in well-drained soil to avoid rot.

LANDSCAPE USE: Flowers to 6 inches (15 cm) tall. Put big sweeps in beds all along your drives and walks or outside your windows so you can enjoy the flower even if you don't spend a lot of time outside in early spring. Use between tree roots where the grass grows thinly and slowly. In shrub or flower gardens, overplant with sweet alyssum (*Lobularia maritima*) or groundcovers to hide the fading foliage.

Dianthus deltoides   Caryophyllaceae

MAIDEN PINKS

Mat-forming maiden pinks are covered with small flowers for most of the summer. Shear the spent bloom stems back to the foliage to encourage additional flowers.

TYPE OF PLANT: Perennial.

SEASON OF INTEREST: Pink, rose, white, or red flowers for most of the summer. The beautiful petals look like they have been notched with pinking shears. The rest of the season you'll enjoy the creeping, evergreen foliage.

BEST CLIMATE AND SITE: Zones 3–9. More vigorous and compact in sun but tolerates light shade; well-drained, reasonably fertile, slightly alkaline soil.

GROWING GUIDELINES: Cut the plants back lightly as soon as they finish flowering to encourage rebloom.

PEST AND DISEASE PREVENTION: Avoid crown rot by planting only in well-drained soil. Don't mulch. Where summers are hot and humid, try single-flowered cultivars, which are less prone to fungal problems.

LANDSCAPE USE: Height to 12 inches (30 cm); width to 24 inches (60 cm). Use a row of it to edge the front of a garden. Set clumps amid other foreground plants in a flower border. Mass it into a colorful groundcover. Use single specimens in a rock garden.

RELATED PLANTS:

COTTAGE PINKS (*D. plumaris*): Perennial; low evergreen leaves and fragrant, often dark-centered, pink or white flowers in early summer.

Dicentra eximia   Fumariaceae

FRINGED BLEEDING HEART

Fringed bleeding heart is an excellent easy-care addition to a moist, shady garden. Dangling, heart-shaped flowers often bloom over the ferny leaves through the summer.

TYPE OF PLANT: Perennial.

SEASON OF INTEREST: Small clusters of heart-shaped pink, purple, and white flowers dangle over divided, blue-tinted leaves from spring to fall in the right site.

BEST CLIMATE AND SITE: Zones 3–8. Light to medium shade; well-drained, moist, rich soil.

GROWING GUIDELINES: Water whenever the soil begins to dry out. Mulch with compost.

PEST AND DISEASE PREVENTION: Plants are generally problem-free.

LANDSCAPE USE: Height to 18 inches (45 cm); slightly narrower spread. It looks good planted in clumps of three or more in woodland gardens. Try combining it with large, blue-leaved hostas and white-flowered impatiens.

RELATED PLANTS:

COMMON BLEEDING HEART (*D. spectabilis*): Has larger flowers on graceful arching branches. Blooms only in spring; goes dormant in summer.

Dictamnus albus   Rutaceae

GAS PLANT

Slow-growing gas plant needs a sunny, well-drained site where it can grow for years without disturbance. In return, you'll get spikes of pink or white summer flowers.

TYPE OF PLANT: Perennial

SEASON OF INTEREST: Dynamic, 1-foot (30 cm) long spikes of white or pink flowers with graceful long stamens on tall stems in early summer. The dark green, lemon-scented foliage is interesting through the rest of the growing season.

BEST CLIMATE AND SITE: Zones 3–8. Full sun; well-drained, deep soil.

GROWING GUIDELINES: Roots dig deep and suffer from disturbance, so plant where it can stay put for years. Because it is slow to start growing in spring, mark the site and keep clear with your hoe or shovel.

PEST AND DISEASE PREVENTION: Plants are generally problem-free.

LANDSCAPE USE: Height to 4 feet (1.2 m); width to 3 feet (90 cm). Use as a lovely upright specimen or in a small group of three. Create even larger masses in the back of a large border.

Echinacea purpurea   Compositae

PURPLE CONEFLOWER

Purple coneflowers form durable clumps that bloom well in both cool and warm climates. The main flush of flowers in midsummer is followed by sporadic blooming until frost.

TYPE OF PLANT: Perennial.

SEASON OF INTEREST: Purple, rose, or white flowers top the distinctively veined foliage from midsummer into fall. The flowers grow to 6 inches (15 cm) across and have orange centers.

BEST CLIMATE AND SITE: Zones 3–8. Sun; well-drained soil of average fertility. Tolerates drier weather and heat.

GROWING GUIDELINES: Can get floppy if you fertilize, especially if you plant it in anything less than full sun. Water during drought. Deadhead to extend the period of bloom.

PEST AND DISEASE PREVENTION: Treating the lawn with milky disease to kill grubs may help avoid Japanese beetle damage.

LANDSCAPE USE: Height 2–4 feet (60–120 cm). Use for an extended period of color in a perennial or meadow garden, although the purplish flower color can be hard to combine with other pink and purple flowers. Try contrasting color combinations with companions like thread-leaved coreopsis (*Coreopsis verticillata*).

Eschscholzia californica Papaveraceae

CALIFORNIA POPPY

Sunny California poppies will thrive on tough, dry or rocky sites. Cut plants back after flowering to promote rebloom or let them self-sow for an informal look.

TYPE OF PLANT: Annual; may be perennial in warm climates.

SEASON OF INTEREST: Bears a rainbow of satiny orange, yellow, red, pink, or white flowers during summer and sometimes into fall.

BEST CLIMATE AND SITE: All Zones. Full sun; well-drained soil. Tolerates dry conditions.

GROWING GUIDELINES: Plant seed directly in your prepared garden bed in early spring. Plants may self-sow. Cut back after the first flush of bloom to encourage rebloom.

PEST AND DISEASE PREVENTION: Plants are generally problem-free.

LANDSCAPE USE: Height to 15 inches (37.5 cm); similar spread. Let it spread casually through flower gardens or meadow gardens. Combine it with sweet alyssum (*Lobularia maritima*) and blue-colored cornflowers (*Centaurea cyanus*).

Eupatorium purpureum Compositae

JOE-PYE WEED

Joe-Pye weed is anything but a weed in the late summer perennial border. Its tall stems are topped with showy domed clusters of purplish flowers that are popular with butterflies.

TYPE OF PLANT: Perennial.

SEASON OF INTEREST: Topped in late summer by rounded clusters of purple or white flowers that grow to 18 inches (45 cm) across.

BEST CLIMATE AND SITE: Zones 4–9, but avoid hot sites. Full sun—it will flop in shade; constantly moist soil.

GROWING GUIDELINES: Deadhead to prevent self-sowing. Water during drought.

PEST AND DISEASE PREVENTION: Plants are generally problem-free.

LANDSCAPE USE: Height 3–6 feet (90–180 cm). A natural for a boggy area. Or grow it in a moist meadow, flower, or cut-flower garden.

RELATED PLANTS:

MIST FLOWER (*E. coelestinum*): An aggressive spreader with blue flower clusters.

Geranium sanguineum Geraniaceae	*Gypsophila paniculata* Caryophyllaceae

BLOOD RED CRANESBILL

BABY'S-BREATH

Low-spreading blood red cranesbill makes a great flowering groundcover for a slope, a flower garden, or a shrub border. Combine it with small bulbs for extra interest.

TYPE OF PLANT: Perennial.

SEASON OF INTEREST: Pink, mauve, or white flowers striped with darker veins in summer. In fall, the attractive, deeply cut leaves turn red.

BEST CLIMATE AND SITE: Zones 3–8. Full sun; light shade in hot sites; well-drained soil.

GROWING GUIDELINES: Cut back lightly after the first flush of flowers to encourage reblooming.

PEST AND DISEASE PREVENTION: Treat the lawn with milky disease to kill beetle grubs and minimize Japanese beetle damage.

LANDSCAPE USE: Height to 12 inches (30 cm); width to 18 inches (45 cm). Makes a good groundcover or edging near the front of a flower or shrub garden. Set spring-flowering bulbs around the perimeter of the plant, which will fill out and hide their fading foliage.

OTHER COMMENTS: The variety *striatum* stays slightly lower and has soft pink flowers.

RELATED PLANTS:

BIGROOT CRANESBILL (*G. macrorrhizum*): Spring-blooming groundcover with soft pink flowers.

ENDRES CRANESBILL (*G. endressi*): Bears prolific numbers of pink flowers in early summer; reaches 18 inches (45 cm) high.

JOHNSON'S BLUE CRANESBILL (*G.* 'Johnson's Blue'): Flowers are more blue than purple; grows 18 inches (45 cm high).

Baby's-breath blooms with clouds of tiny white flowers in summer. Plant it in average to poor soil to prevent succulent, sprawling stems that require staking.

TYPE OF PLANT: Perennial.

SEASON OF INTEREST: A cloud of small white or pink flowers hovers over narrow green-gray leaves during summer.

BEST CLIMATE AND SITE: Zones 3–9. Full sun; well-drained, alkaline to neutral soil of average to low fertility.

GROWING GUIDELINES: Add limestone if your soil is acid. Don't disturb the sensitive roots of this plant or the underground graft union of double-flowered types. Fertilize lightly, if at all, so the flower stems won't get floppy. Cut spent flower stalks to the ground to encourage rebloom.

PEST AND DISEASE PREVENTION: In the right site, generally problem-free.

LANDSCAPE USE: Height to 4 feet (1.2 m). Try in a cut-flower garden or flower border. It can fill gaps left after spring-flowering bulbs or oriental poppies (*Papaver orientale*) die back.

RELATED PLANTS:

CREEPING BABY'S-BREATH (*G. repens*): Grows low to the ground; tolerates slightly acid soils.

Helianthus x *multiflorus*   Compositae

PERENNIAL SUNFLOWER

Perennial sunflowers bear single or double golden flowers in late summer and fall. The tall stems may need staking in windy areas. Cut bloom stems back after flowering.

TYPE OF PLANT: Perennial.

SEASON OF INTEREST: Bears 4-inch (10 cm) wide gold flowers in late summer and fall.

BEST CLIMATE AND SITE: Zones 4–8. Full sun; average soil. Tolerates heat but needs staking in windy sites.

GROWING GUIDELINES: Water when the soil begins to dry out. Cut back the ragged stems after the flowers fade.

PEST AND DISEASE PREVENTION: Use insecticidal soap to control aphids.

LANDSCAPE USE: Height to 5 feet (1.5 m). Allow the plant lots of room. Give it a place to ramble in the back of an informal flower garden or in a cut-flower garden.

RELATED PLANTS:

WILLOW-LEAVED SUNFLOWER (*H. salicifolius*): Height 3–6 feet (90–180 cm). Narrow leaves and golden flowers with purple-brown centers.

Hemerocallis hybrids   Liliaceae

DAYLILIES

Daylilies are among the most dependable perennials for the low-maintenance landscape. These hardy plants bloom in a wide range of colors, heights, and flower forms.

TYPE OF PLANT: Perennial.

SEASON OF INTEREST: Most daylilies flower during summer, but some cultivars bloom in spring, fall, or even winter in warm climates. A few, including 'Stella de Oro', rebloom throughout the growing season. Flowers are yellow, gold, orange, red, pink, or lavender.

BEST CLIMATE AND SITE: Zones 3–9. Full sun; light shade in hot climates; they may not flower well in medium shade. Grow in any kind of soil, as long as it isn't swampy; perform best in well-drained, fertile soil.

GROWING GUIDELINES: Deadhead often if you want a tidy-looking plant. Cut off old flower stalks. Water during drought.

PEST AND DISEASE PREVENTION: Plants are generally problem-free.

LANDSCAPE USE: Height 1–5 feet (30–150 cm), depending on cultivar. Use for almost any landscape need. Mix them with annuals and perennials, or devote an entire garden to different kinds of daylilies. Put compact, long-blooming types like 'Stella de Oro' in planters. Try larger types in meadow gardens, or use them as groundcovers or bank stablilizers.

OTHER COMMENTS: Daylilies with evergreen foliage grow best in warmer climates.

HOSTAS

IMPATIENS

For the shady garden, it's hard to beat hostas for beautiful foliage. The leaves may be wide or narrow; tiny or large; plain green, silver-blue, or marked with yellow or white.

TYPE OF PLANT: Perennial.

SEASON OF INTEREST: Handsome foliage throughout the growing season, although it may get ragged by fall. Depending on the cultivar, foliage color can be green, yellow, blue, or variegated with gold or white. Spikes of purple or white flowers in summer; the blooms of some species are fragrant.

BEST CLIMATE AND SITE: Zones 3–8. A few cultivars can tolerate full sun or deep shade but most thrive in medium shade. Provide moist, well-drained, rich soil.

GROWING GUIDELINES: Mulch plants growing in dry shade to keep soil moist. Remove flower spikes after the flowers fade.

PEST AND DISEASE PREVENTION: Trap slugs and snails by sinking a saucer of beer shallowly in the soil near the plant.

LANDSCAPE USE: Height and width 6–36 inches (15–90 cm), depending on the cultivar. Their leaves can be narrow as a ribbon or broad as a dinner plate. Mingle them with other plants in a shady border or create a mass entirely of hostas.

RELATED PLANTS:

AUGUST LILY (*H. plantaginea*): Broad clumps of heart-shaped green leaves topped with fragrant white flowers in late summer.

Impatiens are popular annuals for adding summer and fall color to shady spots. Choose compact cultivars to get bushy plants without regular pinching.

TYPE OF PLANT: Annual.

SEASON OF INTEREST: Pink, red, orange, and purple flowers—sometimes spotted or striped—during summer and fall in temperate climates or during winter in hot climates. Plants have a graceful mounded shape.

BEST CLIMATE AND SITE: All Zones. Light to medium shade; moist soil.

GROWING GUIDELINES: Plant nursery seedlings at the start of the frost-free growing season. Choose self-branching cultivars available in series such as 'Dazzler Hybrids', 'Starbright Hybrids', and 'Mega Hybrids' to get bushy plants without pinching.

PEST AND DISEASE PREVENTION: Keep the soil cool and moist to avoid spider mites; treat them with insecticidal soap.

LANDSCAPE USE: Height and spread to 2 feet (60 cm). Great bedding plants. Use in masses in shade gardens, under trees, or at the edge of woods. Or plant three or five in smaller clumps of the same color amid other shade plants, like hostas or daylilies. On a shady patio, use in planters or hanging baskets.

RELATED PLANTS:

NEW GUINEA IMPATIENS: More sun-tolerant. Vivid flowers, occasionally combined with variegated or bronze leaves.

Iris sibirica Iridaceae

SIBERIAN IRIS

Siberian iris is a classic part of the early summer perennial border. It thrives in moist soil, although it will adapt to ordinary garden conditions.

TYPE OF PLANT: Perennial.

SEASON OF INTEREST: Sprays of purple, blue, or white beardless flowers in May.

BEST CLIMATE AND SITE: Zones 3–9. Grows best in full sun; tolerates light shade. Thrives in fertile, well-drained soil; can tolerate occasional wet feet.

GROWING GUIDELINES: Water when the soil gets dry. Divide infrequently (only when the plant needs rejuvenation).

PEST AND DISEASE PREVENTION: Plants are generally problem-free.

LANDSCAPE USE: Height 1–3 feet (30–90 cm). Try it in the middle or back of a flower border, perhaps blended with common garden peonies and alumroots (*Heuchera* spp.).

OTHER COMMENTS: Tetraploid forms can have larger flowers.

RELATED PLANTS:

BEARDED IRISES: Flashy flowers, but in return require well-drained soil, frequent division, and constant vigilance for borers and bacterial soft rot.

DANFORD IRIS (*I. danfordiae*): Small yellow flowers in early spring.

Lilium hybrids Liliaceae

LILIES

The bold, colorful blooms make lilies a favorite with many gardeners. Combine them with tall annuals or perennials that can fill in when the lilies are done flowering.

TYPE OF PLANT: Bulb.

SEASON OF INTEREST: Yellow, orange, red, pink, light purple, or white flowers from late spring to late summer (depending on the cultivar). Some cultivars bear clusters of flowers that are 2 inches (5 cm) long; others bear flowers nearly 1 foot (30 cm) long on each stem.

BEST CLIMATE AND SITE: Zones 3–8. Full sun; a few species tolerate light shade. Fertile, moist, well-drained soil.

GROWING GUIDELINES: Plant bulbs in late fall. When flowers emerge in spring, mulch around the stem bases with compost. Fertilize once a month with fish emulsion. Water if the soil begins to get dry during the growing season. Stake taller lilies. Remove faded flowers.

PEST AND DISEASE PREVENTION: Buy disease-free plants. Provide good air circulation and excellent drainage to discourage fungal diseases. Destroy sickly plants and bulbs. Control aphids with insecticidal soap so they cannot spread viral diseases. Since tulips can carry similar viruses, keep the two separate.

LANDSCAPE USE: Height 1–7 feet (30–210 cm). They look good in small groups but leave behind somewhat barren stems after flowering. Try to plant a later-flowering perennial or annual nearby to fill the spot.

Lobelia erinus Campanulaceae

EDGING LOBELIA

Edging lobelia is a colorful, easy-care annual. Try clump-forming cultivars like 'Crystal Palace' in flower beds; use vining types in planters and hanging baskets.

TYPE OF PLANT: Annual.

SEASON OF INTEREST: Vivid violet, blue, or white flowers from late spring through fall if the weather is not too hot. Some cultivars have burgundy-colored leaves.

BEST CLIMATE AND SITE: All Zones. Full sun; light shade in warm climates. Moist, well-drained soil.

GROWING GUIDELINES: Start with nursery plants, or sow seed indoors in late winter. Mulch with compost after planting. Cut back after the first flush of bloom and fertilize with fish emulsion to promote rebloom. Water when the soil begins to dry out.

PEST AND DISEASE PREVENTION: Plants are generally problem-free.

LANDSCAPE USE: Height to 6 inches (15 cm). Use to edge a bed or dangle over the rim of a planter. Set in a rock garden or in the cracks of a stone patio or walk.

OTHER COMMENTS: Choose clump-forming cultivars such as 'Crystal Palace', 'Compacta', and 'Blue Moon' for bedding or vining types such as 'Pendula' and 'Fountain Series' for containers.

RELATED PLANTS:

CARDINAL FLOWER (*L. cardinalis*): Perennial; produces spikes of red flowers in summer.

Lobularia maritima Cruciferae

SWEET ALYSSUM

The fragrant flowers and low, mounding form of sweet alyssum make this annual a great edging or container plant. Try purple- and rose-flowered cultivars for variety.

TYPE OF PLANT: Annual.

SEASON OF INTEREST: Covered with clusters of tiny white flowers throughout the growing season, especially during cooler weather.

BEST CLIMATE AND SITE: All Zones. Full sun or light shade; well-drained soil.

GROWING GUIDELINES: It may be quicker to start from a nursery transplant, but sweet alyssum is also easy to direct-sow in early spring. Once growing, it may self-sow. Cut back lightly after the first flush of bloom to encourage reblooming.

PEST AND DISEASE PREVENTION: Plants are generally problem-free.

LANDSCAPE USE: Height to 4 inches (10 cm). Use this versatile plant along the front edge of a garden bed or let it cascade over the side of a planter. It will fill out to hide fading bulb foliage or soften the barren base of a taller plant. Include it in a garden of self-sowing plants like California poppy (*Eschscholzia californica*), cleome (*Cleome hasslerana*), and cosmos.

OTHER COMMENTS: Purple-flowered sweet alyssum plants can clash with flowers that have different hues of purple and pink. They also are less heat-tolerant than white forms.

Muscari armeniacum   Liliaceae

GRAPE HYACINTH

Plant grape hyacinths in the fall and enjoy their sprightly spring blooms for years to come. Group the bulbs in clumps or drifts to get the most impact.

TYPE OF PLANT: Bulb.

SEASON OF INTEREST: Short spikes of bell-shaped purple, sky blue, or white flowers in early spring.

BEST CLIMATE AND SITE: Zones 2–9. Full sun or light shade; moist, but not wet, soil.

GROWING GUIDELINES: Plant the bulbs 3 inches (7.5 cm) apart and 3 inches (7.5 cm) deep in fall.

PEST AND DISEASE PREVENTION: Plants are generally problem-free.

LANDSCAPE USE: Use in big sweeps of 100 or more under deciduous trees or shrubs or in smaller groups of 10–25 in a rock or flower garden. They look good growing with ajuga (*Ajuga reptans*).

RELATED PLANTS:
M. azureum: Has a thick spike of light blue flowers.
COMMON GRAPE HYACINTH (*M. botryoides*): Bears 12-inch (30 cm) high clusters of blue, white, or pink flowers.

Myosotis sylvatica   Boraginaceae

GARDEN FORGET-ME-NOT

Garden forget-me-nots combine beautifully with spring bulbs. Individual plants may be short-lived but often self-sow prolifically; deadhead if this is a problem.

TYPE OF PLANT: Biennial or perennial.

SEASON OF INTEREST: Fragrant blue flowers with a yellow eye in spring and occasionally afterward. You can also find pink and white forms.

BEST CLIMATE AND SITE: Zones 5–8. Light shade; tolerates full sun in cool climates if the soil is moist.

GROWING GUIDELINES: Sow seed outdoors after frost. Not long-lived but may self-sow if you let the flowers mature.

PEST AND DISEASE PREVENTION: Encourage good air circulation and thin thick growth to reduce rot problems in humid locations.

LANDSCAPE USE: Forms a mound about 6 inches (15 cm) high and wide. Mass in shade or woodland gardens or near water. Let it fill in around fading spring bulbs.

RELATED PLANTS:
FORGET-ME-NOT (*M. scorpioides*): Looks similar but grows in shallow water.

Narcissus spp.   Amaryllidaceae

DAFFODILS

Daffodils are excellent bulbs for the low-maintenance landscape. Plant them in well-drained soil where they'll get sun or light shade, and they'll increase every year.

TYPE OF PLANT: Bulb.

SEASON OF INTEREST: Fragrant gold, orange, white, and even pink and red flowers trumpet the arrival of spring.

BEST CLIMATE AND SITE: Zones 3–9. Sun to light shade; well-drained soil.

GROWING GUIDELINES: Plant the bulbs 6–8 inches (15–20 cm) apart and 6–12 inches (15–30 cm) deep in fall. Remove the flowering stalk after the flowers fade. Leave the foliage until it yellows. Fertilize in early spring with a complete organic fertilizer. Divide if flowering declines because of overcrowding.

PEST AND DISEASE PREVENTION: Plant firm, healthy bulbs in well-drained soil to avoid fungal diseases.

LANDSCAPE USE: Height 6–18 inches (15–45 cm) depending on the cultivar. Use the smallest kinds in rock gardens and larger ones in ornamental gardens. Daffodils make the biggest splash if you plant five, seven, nine, or more of the same cultivar together in a group. Plant even larger masses in woodland or shade gardens or on banks.

RELATED PLANTS:

ANGEL'S-TEARS (*N. triandrus*): Dangling pale yellow or white flowers with reflexed petals.

Paeonia lactiflora   Ranunculaceae

COMMON GARDEN PEONY

Common garden peonies form shrubby clumps of glossy, dark green foliage topped with large blooms in late spring. Tall and double-flowered cultivars may need staking.

TYPE OF PLANT: Perennial.

SEASON OF INTEREST: White, pink, or red single or double flowers in late spring. The petals can spread to 8 inches (20 cm) across. You'll enjoy the glossy, dark foliage through the growing season.

BEST CLIMATE AND SITE: Zones 2–8. Full sun; appreciates light shade in warmer climates but may need staking. Well-drained, fertile soil.

GROWING GUIDELINES: Plant peonies during fall in soil enriched with plenty of organic matter. It's easier to use container-grown nursery transplants; if you have a bareroot plant, set the top of the plant no deeper than 2 inches (5 cm) below the soil surface. In early spring, fertilize with a complete organic fertilizer. Remove the yellowed foliage in fall. Water if the soil begins to dry out.

PEST AND DISEASE PREVENTION: If the weather becomes damp while the plant is flowering, the buds may blacken from Botrytis blight. Destroy the diseased flowers or buds. Destroy the foliage you remove in fall, too.

LANDSCAPE USE: Height and spread to 3 feet (90 cm). Let a single plant stand alone in a flower garden or combine three into a small group.

OTHER COMMENTS: In warm climates, choose single-flowered early cultivars that will bloom before the weather turns too hot, such as 'Burma Ruby', 'America', or 'Vivid Glow'.

Phlox maculata   Polemoniaceae

WILD SWEET WILLIAM

The long flower clusters of wild sweet William bloom atop strong stems in early summer. The glossy, dark green leaves are less prone to mildew than those of garden phlox.

TYPE OF PLANT: Perennial.

SEASON OF INTEREST: White, rose, or mauve flowers in domed clusters in early summer.

BEST CLIMATE AND SITE: Zones 3–9. Full sun; you'll have to stake in light shade. Fertile, moist, well-drained soil.

GROWING GUIDELINES: Fertilize in early spring with compost or a low-nitrogen, organic fertilizer. Too much nitrogen encourages the production of leaves instead of flowers.

PEST AND DISEASE PREVENTION: Avoid spider mites by keeping the soil cool and moist. Control spider mites with insecticidal soap.

LANDSCAPE USE: Height 2–3 feet (60–90 cm). Perfect for grouping in a flower or meadow garden.

OTHER COMMENTS: This species tends to be mildew-resistant.

RELATED PLANTS:

GARDEN PHLOX (*P. paniculata*): Similar growth habit but more susceptible to mildew diseases.

Platycodon grandiflorus   Campanulaceae

BALLOON FLOWER

Grow perennial balloon flower for its curious inflated buds and wide saucer-shaped blooms. In fall, you'll get a bonus as the toothed green leaves turn bright yellow.

TYPE OF PLANT: Perennial.

SEASON OF INTEREST: Produces balloon-like buds during summer that open to upright bell shapes. You can pick from pink, white, or classic violet flowers.

BEST CLIMATE AND SITE: Zones 3–8. Full sun; light shade in warm climates. Well-drained soil.

GROWING GUIDELINES: This plant is slow to emerge in spring; mark its location so you won't dig or hoe into it. Stick with compact selections to avoid staking.

PEST AND DISEASE PREVENTION: Plants are generally problem-free.

LANDSCAPE USE: Height 1–3 feet (30–90 cm), depending on cultivar. Use alone or in small groups in the middle or rear of flower gardens. For contrast, combine with orange coneflowers (*Rudbeckia fulgida*) or daylilies.

OTHER COMMENTS: The variety *mariesii* has blue-violet flowers on stems 12–18 inches tall. 'Apoyama' is a compact cultivar that can grow 6–18 inches (15–95 cm) tall.

Portulaca grandiflora   Portulacaceae

ROSE MOSS

Rose moss will thrive in those hot, dry, rocky conditions that cause most annuals to shrivel and die. The colorful flowers tend to close at night and during cloudy days.

TYPE OF PLANT: Annual.

SEASON OF INTEREST: Unveils single or double white, red, pink, yellow, or orange flowers that look like little roses through the summer and fall.

BEST CLIMATE AND SITE: All Zones. Full sun; well-drained soil. Tolerates sandy soil and drought.

GROWING GUIDELINES: Start with nursery transplants. They may self-sow once established.

PEST AND DISEASE PREVENTION: Plants are generally problem-free.

LANDSCAPE USE: Height to 8 inches (20 cm). Use in hot, dry locations such as between stones in walls, walks, or patios, or in sunny planters. You can also sprinkle it around rock gardens or fading spring bulbs.

Rudbeckia fulgida   Compositae

ORANGE CONEFLOWER

A mass of orange coneflowers makes an eye-catching show on a sunny bank or in a late summer border. Leave the seed heads for winter interest or deadhead to prevent self-sowing.

TYPE OF PLANT: Perennial.

SEASON OF INTEREST: Gold daisy-like flowers with dark central cones during summer and fall.

BEST CLIMATE AND SITE: Zones 3–9. Full sun; well-drained soil. Tolerates drought.

GROWING GUIDELINES: Start with divisions or nursery transplants. Deadhead after flowering or leave the seed heads on for winter interest and self-sown seedlings. Divide every 4 years to renew.

PEST AND DISEASE PREVENTION: Plants are generally problem-free.

LANDSCAPE USE: Height to 3 feet (90 cm). Use in a wild meadow garden or civilized flower garden. Set clumps of three in a shrub border or mass 25 or more on a bank. Some good companions include 'Autumn Joy' sedum (_Sedum_ 'Autumn Joy') and violet sage (_Salvia_ x _superba_).

OTHER COMMENTS: 'Goldsturm' black-eyed Susan (_R. fulgida_ var. _sullivantii_ 'Goldsturm') is a compact and especially long-blooming selection.

RELATED PLANTS:

BLACK-EYED SUSAN (_R. hirta_): Annual. Large gold flowers and purplish brown central cones.

Salvia x *superba*   Labiatae

VIOLET SAGE

Long-blooming violet sage produces showy spikes of purplish, blue, or rose-colored flowers for most of the summer. Remove old flower spikes to promote rebloom in fall.

TYPE OF PLANT: Perennial.

SEASON OF INTEREST: Slim spikes of violet, blue, or rose flowers from midsummer and occasionally into fall.

BEST CLIMATE AND SITE: Zones 4–7. Full sun; well-drained, moist soil.

GROWING GUIDELINES: Water when the soil begins to dry out. Deadhead promptly to encourage rebloom. Divide every 4 years to renew. In warm climates, use lower-growing cultivars to avoid staking.

PEST AND DISEASE PREVENTION: Plants are generally problem-free.

LANDSCAPE USE: Height 18–36 inches (45–90 cm). Use in clumps of five, seven, or nine in flower borders. Also excellent for use as cut flowers.

OTHER COMMENTS: Many excellent cultivars are available. 'Blue Queen' grows to 2 feet (60 cm) tall with violet-blue flowers. More-compact 'East Friesland' has deep purple flowers on 18-inch (45 cm stems).

Scilla sibirica   Liliaceae

SIBERIAN SQUILL

Siberian squills may look delicate, but they are easy to grow in sun or light shade and average soil. Combine them with groundcovers to fill in when the bulbs go dormant.

TYPE OF PLANT: Bulb.

SEASON OF INTEREST: Vivid blue or white flowers in early spring.

BEST CLIMATE AND SITE: Zones 2–8. Full sun or light shade; well-drained soil.

GROWING GUIDELINES: Plant the bulbs 3 inches (7.5 cm) apart and 3 inches (7.5 cm) deep in fall. Leave the foliage on until it yellows.

PEST AND DISEASE PREVENTION: Provide good drainage to avoid crown rot.

LANDSCAPE USE: Height 3–6 inches (7.5–15 cm). Use in large drifts. Place it near your walk, driveway, or window so you can enjoy the color even if you don't spend a lot of time outdoors in early spring. Combine Siberian squill with groundcovers like spotted lamium (*Lamium maculatum*) that can hide the ripening bulb foliage.

| *Sedum spectabile* | Crassulaceae | *Tropaeolum majus* | Tropaeolaceae |

SHOWY STONECROP

GARDEN NASTURTIUM

Perennial showy stonecrop bears clusters of pink flowers in late summer. Plants may flop in shade or rich soil; pinch stems in spring to promote stronger growth.

Bright-flowered garden nasturtiums will add loads of color to a sunny bed or container planting. They may tolerate heat, but they grow best in cool, humid climates.

TYPE OF PLANT: Perennial.

SEASON OF INTEREST: Green flower buds that resemble heads of broccoli in midsummer. The flowers open pink in late summer and turn crimson as they mature in fall. Leave the flower stems up in winter to enjoy the silhouette.

BEST CLIMATE AND SITE: Zones 3–10. Full sun; well-drained soil. Tolerates drought.

GROWING GUIDELINES: Pinch in early spring to keep the plant from flopping open in the center.

PEST AND DISEASE PREVENTION: Plants are generally problem-free.

LANDSCAPE USE: Height and width to 2 feet (60 cm). Use in clumps or large sweeps in any flower garden.

OTHER COMMENTS: 'Autumn Joy' is a popular hybrid with strong stems and darker flowers; 'Variegatum' (also sold as *S. alboroseum* 'Medio-variegatus') has variegated foliage.

RELATED PLANTS: See the Kamschatka sedum (*S. kamtschaticum*) entry on page 56.

TYPE OF PLANT: Annual.

SEASON OF INTEREST: Interesting spurred, or occasionally flat-backed, orange, yellow, or red flowers from summer into fall.

BEST CLIMATE AND SITE: Zones 3–9. Full sun; average soil.

GROWING GUIDELINES: Direct-sow seed at the start of the frost-free growing season.

PEST AND DISEASE PREVENTION: Use insecticidal soap to control aphids.

LANDSCAPE USE: Bedding nasturtiums such as 'Alaska' and 'Whilybird' grow about 14 inches (35 cm) high; vining types such as 'Park's Fragrant Giant' or 'Climbing Mixed' can stretch to 8 feet (2.4 m) long. Use bedding types near vegetable or herb gardens. Try the peppery flowers and leaves in salads. Let vining types climb a trellis or stone wall.

RELATED PLANTS:

CANARY CREEPER (*T. peregrinum*): Yellow flowers on 6-foot (1.8 m) long stems.

| *Tulipa kaufmanniana* | Liliaceae | *Yucca filamentosa* | Agavaceae |

KAUFMANNIANA TULIP

ADAM'S-NEEDLE

If you want a good show of tulips without having to replant each year, try the perennial Kaufmanniana tulip. Its starry flowers close at night and open each morning.

TYPE OF PLANT: Bulb.

SEASON OF INTEREST: White, pink, and green flowers in early spring. The leaves may be mottled.

BEST CLIMATE AND SITE: Zones 3–8. Full sun; well-drained, fertile soil.

GROWING GUIDELINES: Plant the bulbs 2–4 inches (5–10 cm) apart and 4–6 inches (10–15 cm) deep in fall. Fertilize with a balanced organic fertilizer in early spring. Deadhead promptly. Leave the foliage on until it yellows.

PEST AND DISEASE PREVENTION: Plant disease-free bulbs in well-drained soil.

LANDSCAPE USE: Height to 8 inches (20 cm). Use in rock gardens, shrub borders, or anywhere you'll see it early in spring.

RELATED PLANTS: Many excellent species tulips can live longer than the hybrids. They include:

FOSTERIANA TULIP (*T. fosteriana*): Bright red flowers that grow to 10 inches (25 cm) high.

GREIGII TULIP (*T. greggii*): Mottled foliage; red, yellow, or orange flowers that grow to 8 inches (20 cm) high.

Adam's-needle forms striking evergreen rosettes of spiky leaves topped with large white flowers. Well-drained soil is a must for this tough, drought-tolerant perennial.

TYPE OF PLANT: Woody perennial.

SEASON OF INTEREST: Towering stems of white, bell-shaped flowers shoot up above spiky, evergreen leaves in summer.

BEST CLIMATE AND SITE: Zones 4–10. Full sun; well-drained soil. Tolerates drought.

GROWING GUIDELINES: Deadhead flowers after blooming.

PEST AND DISEASE PREVENTION: Plant in loose, well-drained soil to avoid rot.

LANDSCAPE USE: Use a single plant as a specimen in a flower garden or cluster three together in a shrub grouping.

OTHER COMMENTS: The cultivar 'Bright Edge' has yellow-variegated leaves.

RELATED PLANTS:

SPANISH-DAGGER (*Y. gloriosa*): Hardy in Zones 7–10; greenish to red flowers in summer.

EFFORTLESS EDIBLES

Anyone who has eaten really fresh produce knows that a food-producing garden is worth the effort, even if you have to toil for hours every day under a burning sun. Fortunately, you can enjoy fresh, homegrown vegetables, herbs, and berries with a minimum of toil and trouble.

The trick to low-maintenance food gardening is to be realistic about what and how much you can grow. The best strategy is to start small. Choose a few of the crops that you like best, and plant a limited quantity of each. (Maybe only one each of large plants like zucchini or cucumbers, two or three each of tomatoes and peppers, and six to eight plants each of smaller crops like lettuce and beans.) In following years, adjust the amounts based on how much you used this year.

Another aspect of low maintenance is growing crops that are adapted to your garden. Many vegetables, herbs, and fruits are adapted to a wide range of climates and conditions. But some food plants do have special requirements that may make them tricky to grow in your garden. Carrots need a deep sandy soil to stretch out in, so if your garden is clay or rock, skip them or build raised beds. Cool-loving rhubarb gets spindly in hot climates, while heat-loving melon can be a real disappointment in cool-summer areas.

Even if you eliminate all of the more fussy species, though, there is still a wide range of plants to choose from for almost any site. How can you decide what is best to grow? In many states, the Cooperative Extension Service tests vegetables and small fruit cultivars and publishes lists with their recommendations. They may also put out a booklet explaining how to grow vegetables and fruits in your area. All-America Selections (AAS) also tests and recommends new cultivars of vegetables (flowers, too) that perform outstandingly well. This nonprofit group has test gardens all over the country, so a cultivar that receives an AAS recommendation is likely to do well in your garden, too. Look for the red, white, and blue AAS shield next to catalog entries or on seed packets.

Another consideration to keep in mind when you're choosing plants is insect and disease resistance. Crops that are naturally less susceptible to pest problems mean less work and higher yields for you. Most herbs are naturally pest-resistant. For small fruit, the best way to get healthy plants is to buy from suppliers with certified disease-free stock.

In this chapter, you'll learn the simple steps for growing easy edible crops. "The Low-maintenance Vegetable Garden" on page 126 covers the basics of planning for minimal work while still getting good yields. "Garden Care through the Year" on page 130 walks you through the simple seasonal maintenance steps for healthy, productive herb and vegetable gardens. "Easy Herb Gardens" on page 134 discusses how to incorporate these low-care plants into your landscape. "Low-maintenance Fruits and Berries" on page 136 discusses easy-care fruit crops that can give you bountiful harvests with minimal care. For detailed information on growing specific vegetables, herbs, and fruit crops, see "Low-maintenance Edibles," starting on page 138.

Opposite: Even a low-maintenance landscape can provide loads of fresh produce all season long. Choose easy-to-grow crops like brambles, buy plants adapted to your climate, and give them the best possible growing conditions.

The Low-maintenance Vegetable Garden

Like other parts of the low-maintenance landscape, the easy-care vegetable garden starts with a plan. Knowing what you want to grow will help you decide when to plant and how much maintenance you'll have to do. But there are many other ways planning can reduce overall vegetable maintenance, no matter what you want to grow. To learn how to care for your crops after planting, see "Garden Care through the Year" on page 130.

Selecting the Right Site

Starting with a good site is a vital part of making a low-maintenance garden. Most vegetables grow best where they get a full day of sun (usually on the south or west side of your house). Some, like lettuce, peas, and spinach, will get by with only 6 hours of sun. But in most cases, vegetables without enough light will yield poorly and be more prone to pest and disease problems. Water and nutrient deficiencies can be a problem, too, if your crops have to compete with the roots of the trees that are casting the shade.

Other site considerations include drainage, access to water, and access by equipment. Vegetables prefer a steady supply of soil moisture—not too much or too little. A slightly sloping spot will usually provide ideal drainage. Level sites can be fine, but avoid low spots where water collects during rains, especially if your soil tends to be on the clayey side. (If you have no other choice but to garden on poorly drained soil, consider building raised beds, as explained in the "Landscape Solutions Guide," starting on page 28.)

Make sure you have easy access to a water source, in

A well-organized vegetable garden can be an attractive and functional part of even the smallest yard.

case natural rainfall is deficient. Ideally, you'd have a permanent irrigation system that would turn itself on automatically. If you're not that lucky, make sure that you can easily reach the garden with hoses. It can be a real pain to haul hoses around, but it's a far sight easier than lugging individual buckets!

Also consider the equipment you might be using as you choose a site. Make sure you have easy access to the site with at least a wheelbarrow or garden cart. For many low-maintenance gardeners, tiller access is also critical. Plan for easy access now, and you'll avoid many maintenance headaches in the future.

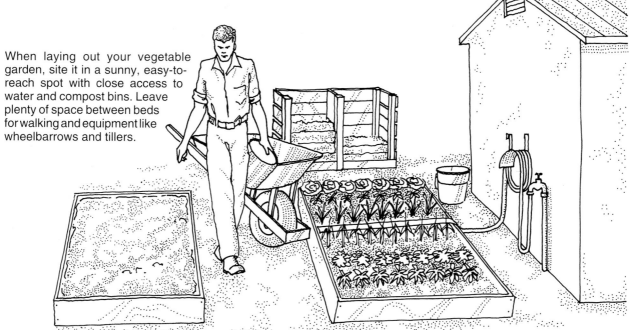

When laying out your vegetable garden, site it in a sunny, easy-to-reach spot with close access to water and compost bins. Leave plenty of space between beds for walking and equipment like wheelbarrows and tillers.

Rows are easy to plan and plant, but they may need more frequent weeding and watering due to the exposed soil.

Picking a Planting Pattern

Once you've chosen the best site, think about how you want to arrange your plantings. Parallel rows are easy to plan and plant, but they're not necessarily easy to maintain. Since lots of soil is exposed, you'll probably need to weed and water more often, unless you mulch early and heavily.

Planting in beds is a much more efficient use of garden space. Since plants are closer together, you'll do less weeding and get higher yields from small areas. The beds do take some time to make the first year (see the "Landscape Solutions Guide," starting on page 28, for tips on constructing raised beds). But in following years, you can concentrate your soil-improvement efforts there instead of working up the whole garden area.

Choosing Your Crops

Deciding what you'll grow is one of the most fun parts of garden planning. The best way to start is to list the vegetables you like to eat already. Then if lack of time or garden space must limit what you grow, you will have to make some choices. If you just can't live without fresh sweet corn, for

instance, you may decide to devote all your available time and space for one short but glorious harvest. If you'd rather grow a variety of vegetables but still have a minimum of work, concentrate on crops that will bear over a long season. Pole beans, peppers, carrots, cucumbers, summer squash, and tomatoes can yield produce over a period of weeks or months from a single planting. As a bonus, they produce slowly but steadily, so you won't have to be out harvesting every day or be swamped by an excess of produce at one time. "Hints for Better Harvests" on page 128 covers maintenance considerations for many popular vegetables.

When you go to buy your vegetable seeds and plants, you'll often have a choice between several different cultivars of the same crop. Cultivars can vary widely in characteristics like heat tolerance, size, and disease resistance. If your garden is in a particularly cool or hot area, it's smart to select cultivars adapted to those extremes. Insect and disease tolerance can be useful if you've had problems with that crop in the past. Compact and bush cultivars can be real time-savers, since you can get the same yields with fewer plants that take up less space. When choosing tomatoes, look for cultivars labeled "indeterminate": They'll produce a steady supply of fruit throughout the season. Determinate tomatoes are more compact, but their fruit ripens all at once.

If space is limited, look for bush or compact cultivars of squash and other favorite crops. You can get high yields from just a few plants in a small garden.

Deciding between Seeds and Transplants

Many vegetables, including cucumbers, corn, lettuce, radishes, carrots, and beans, are easy to grow from seed sown directly in the garden. Others, though—like tomatoes and peppers—germinate poorly in the soil or grow too slowly if you direct-sow the seed. These crops need to be set out as transplants. If you want to grow these crops, you must decide whether to buy the transplants or start the seed yourself.

It's far easier to let a commercial grower raise the transplants from seed—all you have to do is pick them out at the garden center and pay for them. One disadvantage of buying transplants is that you spend slightly more per plant than if you grew your own. Another is that you have fewer cultivars to choose from. Of the hundreds of tomato cultivars on the market, for example, you may find only half a dozen offered for sale as transplants. If you desperately want to try cultivars that you can't find at the garden center, grow your own from seed. But if you really want to keep the fuss and muss to a minimum, it's worth the slight extra initial cost to buy transplants.

If you're willing to pay a little extra, you can save yourself a lot of time by starting with transplants.

Hints for Better Harvests

Here are some tips for getting the highest or longest yield for the least amount of work.

Beans: To get a steady supply of bush beans, instead of massive quantities that have to be picked all at once, plant successive crops at 7- to 10-day intervals. Or try pole beans—they grow tall, so you have to set up a tripod of stakes for them to twine around, but they'll produce for a long season from a single planting. And you don't have to stoop to pick them!

Broccoli: For a longer harvest, look for cultivars like 'Packman' and 'Goliath' that will produce smaller side shoots after you harvest the main head.

Carrots: Sow more thickly than usual, and harvest some of the thinnings for eating each week.

Corn: Plant successive crops every 7 to 10 days for a more even yield.

Cucumbers: Choose bush cultivars to get a high yield from a small space.

Lettuce: If summer heat stops spring sowings early, try late-summer plantings for harvesting well into fall.

Peas: Like lettuce, peas may stop producing when summer's heat starts. Late-summer plantings will extend the pea season into fall.

Peppers: If your peppers stop producing in midsummer, don't pull them out—they'll often set more fruit when slightly cooler weather comes.

Squash: Like cucumbers, squash are available in bush cultivars that offer high yields from limited growing space.

Tomatoes: Some gardeners carefully stake and prune their tomatoes, but you don't have to. It's all right to let the plants grow on the ground. They'll take up more space and you'll have to wash the tomatoes, but they're much less work. Or set up cages around the young plants, and let the cages support the stems.

Cabbage is a particularly cold-tolerant crop. Set seedlings out about 4 weeks before the last spring frost.

Squash plants are very cold-sensitive, especially when young. Sow seed several weeks after the last frost.

Starting a Schedule

Once you decide what to grow, make a planting schedule for the upcoming season. Jot down the planting dates for your chosen crops on a calendar or in a special gardening notebook. The schedule will remind you when to shop for seeds or transplants, so you can buy the things you need at the right time.

How early you can start planting depends on the frost tolerance of the crops you've chosen. At right is a simple timetable for planting some common crops into the garden. (If you're not sure of the average date of the last frost in your area, ask gardening neighbors or your local Cooperative Extension Service.)

- **4 to 6 weeks before last frost date:** Very hardy vegetables such as pea (seeds), onion (sets), and spinach (seeds).
- **2 to 4 weeks before last frost date:** Hardy vegetables such as carrot (seeds) and celery (transplants).
- **Last frost date:** Tender vegetables like tomato (transplants) and beans (seeds).
- **2 to 3 weeks after last frost date:** Very tender vegetables like cucumber (seeds or transplants) and green pepper (transplants).

Set out tomato transplants and sow beans around the last frost date.

Sow peas and spinach and plant onion sets 4 to 6 weeks before the last frost date.

Sow carrots and set out celery transplants 2 to 4 weeks before the last frost.

Wait until 2 to 3 weeks after the last frost date to set out cucumbers and peppers.

Garden Care through the Year

Vegetables do require more work than almost any other landscape plant, but they will also reward you with quantities of tasty produce. Follow the simple care calendar below, and your crops will thrive with a minimum of fuss.

Winter

For low-maintenance gardeners, winter can be as important as any other season. The planning you do on these long winter nights will help you prevent problems later on. This is the time to decide what you want to grow and how much you are going to plant. As you search through seed catalogs, look for compact, high-yielding vegetable cultivars that will provide a bountiful harvest in a small space. Also consider cultivars that are insect- or disease-resistant, so you'll have fewer pest problems to cope with. Order your seeds now, and save yourself a trip to the garden center later on. This is also a good time to plan the planting schedule so you'll put your crops in at the right time for best growth. For more tips on planning for easy-care crops, see "The Low-maintenance Vegetable Garden" on page 126.

Spring

The weather's getting warmer, the spring bulbs are in full bloom, and you've got the itch to get your vegetable garden going. But before you start digging, take a few minutes to review the plans you made during the

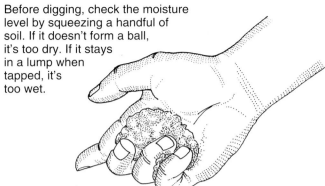

Before digging, check the moisture level by squeezing a handful of soil. If it doesn't form a ball, it's too dry. If it stays in a lump when tapped, it's too wet.

winter. Check your planting schedule to see what crops should go in first. Get out the seeds you ordered, or take your shopping list to the garden center and buy the seeds, transplants, and other supplies that you need. Don't be tempted to buy extra plants or plants that aren't on your list. You'll either end up cramming the extras in with the others or digging new beds to accommodate them. Either way, you'll end up with much more maintenance than you planned for.

Soil Preparation The first time you ever prepare your garden you'll need to till or dig the whole thing to remove the grass and weeds, loosen the soil, work in organic matter, and remove buried rocks. By doing a good job the first year, future planting will be easy: Instead of tilling the entire garden, you can just dig a row for seeds and a hole for each transplant.

Keep your soil in good shape by not working it when

Keeping your gardening tools and equipment organized may seem like extra work, but it will save you time in the long run. You won't have to waste minutes rummaging around for a misplaced trowel or hours searching for that book you need.

Mulching is a key part of a low-maintenance vegetable garden. It reduces the need for water and keeps weeds down.

When sowing seed directly into the garden, use a rake to smooth the surface and form a fine seedbed.

it's too wet or too dry. To check soil moisture, try this simple test: Take a handful of the soil, and squeeze it into a ball. If the soil won't make a ball, it's probably too dry. Water the area thoroughly, and wait a day or two before digging. If the soil does stick together, tap the ball with a finger. If the ball falls apart, it's safe to work the soil. If the soil stays in a lump, it's too wet. Wait a few days, and try the test again.

Planting For direct-sown seed, loosen the soil in the area you're going to plant, rake it, and firm it gently. Sprinkle the seed evenly over the bed, or plant in straight rows. Keep the seedbed evenly moist until the seeds sprout.

For transplants, loosen the soil in an area slightly bigger than the transplant's root ball. Set the plant in the hole and fill in around the roots with soil. Keep transplants well watered until they start showing new growth.

To help your plants be as vigorous as possible and to make working among them easier, be sure to space them properly. The seed packet or plant tag gives the correct spacing distance. If you sow seeds too thickly, they'll come up crowded and you'll have to thin them out by pulling out the smaller seedlings and leaving the strongest ones at an even spacing.

Summer

This season is the time that your winter planning and spring planting pay off. As your vegetables and herbs mature in the warm summer weather, a little extra attention can keep yields high and routine maintenance minimal.

Mulching Mulches are the cornerstone to low-maintenance vegetables and herbs. Mulches help keep critical moisture in the soil and moderate temperature extremes for better root growth. They reduce weeding chores by smothering weed seeds. Mulches keep soil from splashing onto plants, reducing the spread of soilborne diseases and keeping herbs and produce cleaner. And as they break down, organic mulches release a balanced supply of plant nutrients and add organic matter to improve soil structure.

While dozens of materials are used as mulches, not all of them are equally good at doing all the things mulches can do. Compost is a great all-around mulch that adds nutrients and organic matter, although it will not suppress perennial weeds such as johnsongrass or Canada thistle. Grass clippings and weed-free straw are other excellent multi-purpose mulches, but they will not smother perennial weeds either. Newspaper, on the other hand, is dense enough to block most weeds, and it eventually breaks down to add organic matter to the soil (although not necessarily in one season). Newspaper's drawback is that it blows around unless you anchor it with rocks or another mulch. Black plastic mulch is commonly used in vegetable gardens to smother weeds and retain soil moisture, but it won't add any nutrients or organic matter to the soil. In many cases, the best solution is to use a combination of mulches to get the best of each.

Whichever mulch or combination you choose, always weed thoroughly before applying it. (In most cases, covering existing weeds with mulch will not get rid of them.) If you're using black plastic or newspaper, lay it on either side of seedling rows. Or if you're using transplants, spread the material over the planting area, and cut holes so you can plant right through it. When applying loose organic mulches (like compost or straw), wait until direct-sown seedlings are about 6 inches (15 cm) tall or your transplants are in the ground. Lay down a 1- to 3-inch (2.5 to 7.5 cm) layer of mulch. Keep organic mulches about 1 inch (2.5 cm) away from plant stems to discourage rot.

Watering Mulches save water, but not enough that you can forget about watering. A general rule of thumb is that most crops need 1 inch (25 mm) of water a week, from rain or irrigation. But what really matters is how moist the soil is. If it hasn't rained for a few days, dig down 2 to 3 inches (5 to 7.5 cm) into the soil. If that soil feels moist, wait a few days and check again. If the soil is dry, it's time to water.

Water slowly and deeply to encourage deep roots that don't get stressed easily during hot, dry weather. With a sprinkler, this could take several hours. Soaker hoses, which ooze water evenly along their length, are easy to install, and they save water by delivering it right to the soil. (Plus it can take less time to water, since you're only irrigating the plants that really need it rather than the whole garden.) For the ultimate easy maintenance, install an automatic drip irrigation system. (See page 29 for more information on planning and using an irrigation system.)

Weeding Pull or dig up the weeds that make it through the mulch, preferably while they're tiny. If for some reason a weed makes it to adulthood, be sure to

If rabbits are a problem, surround your crops with a wire-mesh fence that is partially sunken into the soil.

yank it before it sets seed, so you don't have to contend with its more numerous offspring next year.

Fertilizing If you've done a good job preparing the soil and working in ample amounts of organic matter, the layer of compost or aged manure you put down each year is enough to replenish the nutrients your vegetables remove from the soil.

Some gardeners like to give their vegetables an additional boost around midsummer. You can apply a liquid fertilizer such as fish emulsion or seaweed by either pouring it on the soil or spraying it on the leaves. You can also scratch a balanced dry organic fertilizer into the soil around the plant (pull back the mulch first, apply the fertilizer, then replace the mulch).

Managing Pests The low-maintenance way to manage insects and diseases is usually to tolerate them. Few pests do enough damage to reduce your harvest noticeably. If you leave pest insects alone, you'll encourage beneficial insects that prey on them and keep their populations in check. Covering crops with pest barriers like floating row covers is another low-maintenance pest-control option. You can prevent many diseases by cleaning up plant litter, spacing plants properly, and growing disease-resistant cultivars.

Rabbits and other creatures are another matter; they can do serious damage. The surest deterrent is to encircle your vegetable garden with a fence that's about 2 feet (60 cm) high. Bend the bottom 6 inches (15 cm) out at an angle, and bury the bottom 2 inches (5 cm)

Growing flowers and herbs in your vegetable garden will help to attract beneficial, pest-eating insects.

below ground. Rabbits won't be able to dig under it because they'll be standing on the buried section, and they won't be able to jump over it because it's too high.

While fencing may seem like an extreme solution, it's one you can rely on every year. Other methods, such as scattering human or pet hair around plants or dusting crops with hot pepper powder, only work sometimes. And having to keep trying new repellents is more work in the long run.

Fall

As the lower temperatures of fall arrive, many vegetables that took a break during the summer heat will put on new growth or set more fruit. Late summer plantings of crops like peas and lettuce can yield well into the fall season, when the cool weather makes picking a pleasure rather than a chore.

Fall Cleanup Once your crops are done for the season, spend a few minutes putting the garden to bed so it will be ready for spring planting next season. In addition to making the garden look tidier during the winter, picking up dead plants and dropped vegetables eliminates hiding places for insect eggs and disease pathogens. (Add seed- and disease-free materials to your compost pile; bury seedy or diseased plants or dispose of them with your household trash.) While you're at it, pull up and clean off any metal or wooden stakes and stick them in the garage so they don't rust or rot. Finally, wash all your tools and wipe a light coating of oil on them before storing.

Compost for Busy People

Composting fits well into a timesaving scheme. For one thing, it saves you a chore in the evenings—instead of taking your kitchen scraps out to garbage, then heading to the garden to check on things, you can dump the scraps in the pile near the garden and skip the garbage trip. And later you can use the compost for fertilizer and mulch, saving you a trip to the garden center.

For easy access, put your compost pile on a level, well-drained spot close to the garden. Some gardeners build elaborate, multichambered compost bins. You can get by, however, by just dumping your stuff in a pile. Besides kitchen scraps, you can toss in pulled weeds, if they don't have seeds. You can add grass clippings that you raked up to keep from smothering your lawn. You can add fresh manure, sawdust, shredded paper from the office paper shredder—just about any plant or plant derivative will work. Don't add diseased plants because the bacteria, fungi, or viruses might survive. Meats, fat, and bones are undesirable because they attract animals. And don't add dog or cat manures, which can harbor diseases.

Turn the pile every so often with a pitchfork—the more often you turn it, the more air gets in it and the faster the soil organisms can break it down. If you're chronically pressed for time, buy a cheap pitchfork and leave it near the compost pile so you can turn the pile when the mood strikes, not on those less-frequent occasions when you remember to bring the good fork from the garage. When your compost is dark and crumbly (in a few weeks or months), it's ready to use.

A small herb garden is easy to care for, and it can provide plenty of material for cooking, crafts, or drying.

Easy Herb Gardens

Herbs are great for low-maintenance landscapes. These versatile plants can adapt to lots of different sites and will thrive with minimal care.

Choosing Easy-care Herbs

There are so many wonderful herbs that it can be hard to decide which ones to grow. Some herbs, like oregano and peppermint, are used in cooking or for tea; others, like lavender and sage, are ideal for potpourris and other fragrant crafts. Some herbs, like bee balm, thyme, and yarrow, are attractive in their own right as ornamentals, even if you never plan to harvest them for any purpose. Many herbs fall into more than one of these categories.

How you plan to use your herbs will affect how you'll grow them and how much attention they'll need from you. If you're just growing herbs to use fresh in cooking, you don't need much space for an herb garden, since one or two plants of each kind you like should be enough. You'll be most likely to use your culinary herbs if you plant them close to the house. If you're only growing one

Chives are popular for their mild onion-flavored leaves and flowers. Remove spent blooms.

Helpful Hints for Easy Herbs

Before you decide which herbs you want to grow, check out their maintenance considerations below.

Basil: For best leaf production, pick off flower heads as they form (every few days). May also need extra water.

Chives: Easy to grow, but can reseed prolifically if you don't clip off spent flowers.

Dill: Let a few plants self-sow the first year, and you'll probably never need to replant. Pull seedlings from where they're not wanted. Or remove flowers if you don't want seedlings.

Mints: Most tend to spread rapidly unless contained. Plant in bottomless pots sunk in the soil to 1 inch (2.5 cm) below the rim. Or grow as container plants.

Parsley: Seeds are slow to germinate and seedlings can get swamped by weeds. Often easiest to start from transplants.

Rosemary: In cold climates, treat as an annual and buy new plants each year.

Sage: Start from transplants; easy to grow.

Thyme: Won't compete well with weeds, so keep weeded until plants get established.

or two types, try growing them in large pots on the deck or patio. You'll need more space to grow quantities of herbs if you plan to harvest them for drying and crafting. "Helpful Hints for Easy Herbs" offers maintenance tips for many popular cooking and craft herbs.

Growing Your Herbs

Most herbs prefer full sun, although some (like sweet woodruff, chervil, lemon balm, and many mints) will grow in partial shade. Many herbs tolerate rocky, thin soils, but they will be more productive in average, well-drained soil. You may choose to plant your herbs in a separate garden, but they also look great mixed into flower beds and vegetable gardens.

You can grow many herbs—including such favorites as dill, sage, marjoram, and basil—from seed sown

A small container planting can provide easy-to-pick sprigs of parsley and basil for the hurried cook.

directly in the garden. Other herbs are easier to grow from transplants than seeds; these include rosemary, lavender, peppermint, and tarragon, among others. For the most part, the vegetable-growing information covered in "Garden Care through the Year" on page 130 applies equally well to herbs. One exception is that many herbs, including rosemary, marjoram, oregano, sage, and thyme, grow best with little or no mulch, so you'll need to pay closer attention to weeding these.

Harvesting Herbs

When you harvest leaves, try to pick them early in the day, when the oils are most concentrated and the flavors most intense. Your herbs will produce more foliage if you pinch off the flower heads as they develop. But if you're growing the herb for seed (like dill or caraway), leave the flower head and harvest the seed after it turns

Herb gardens can be beautiful as well as useful. Mix in a variety of herbs that have colorful leaves and flowers.

Preserving Herbs the Easy Way

Extend your enjoyment of your herbs into the winter season by preserving them for crafts or culinary use. Try one of these methods:

Bag Drying Separate the herbs into small bunches. Twist a string or rubber band around the base of the stems on each bunch. Place each bunch upside down in a paper bag, gathering and tying the bag's opening around the base of the stems. Hang the plants upside down in a warm, dry place until the leaves dry out (about a week or two).

Tray Drying Spread clean leaves in a single layer on a mesh screen and let them air dry in a warm, dry place for about a week.

Oven Drying Spread clean leaves on a cookie sheet and dry in a warm (100°F/38°C) oven with the door open for about 2 hours.

Freezing Store culinary herbs in a small resealable plastic bag. Label the bag and toss it in the freezer; remove frozen herbs as needed for cooking.

After bag-, tray-, or oven-drying, store herbs in an airtight jar or resealable plastic bag in a cool, dark place to retain the best flavor and color.

Dry herbs by hanging them upside down in a brown paper bag.

For fast drying, spread leaves on a cookie sheet and dry in the oven.

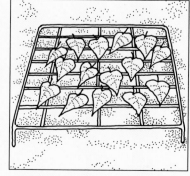

Or spread individual leaves in a single layer on a screen to air-dry.

Low-maintenance Fruits and Berries

Growing fruit is slightly more complicated than growing flowers or vegetables, but the rewards can make it all worthwhile. If you really want low maintenance, stick with the simplest fruit crops, like brambles, blueberries, and strawberries. These plants are generally easy to maintain without a lot of pruning or pest control. Fruit trees like apples, peaches, and pears really aren't ideal for low-maintenance landscapes unless you want to reduce other garden chores to have more time for growing more labor-intensive fruit.

Below you'll find tips for success with some of the easiest fruit crops. For more information on these and other fruiting plants, check out "Low-maintenance Edibles," starting on page 138.

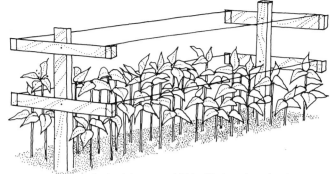

A double-armed T-trellis is a handy structure for keeping brambles contained and easy to pick. Remove the side wires for easy access at pruning time.

Backyard Brambles

For low-maintenance gardeners, brambles like raspberries and blackberries are a productive and rewarding crop. These easy-to-grow plants can live as long as 10 years, so choose and prepare the site carefully. Brambles need full sun and should be far from their wild cousins, which might carry disease. Choose a well-drained site or build a raised bed.

To save space and make harvesting easier, train brambles to a trellis. The double-armed T is an easy system. At either end of the bed, set in two vertical posts as tall as the mature plant will be. On each post, attach two horizontal bars, one in the middle and one at the top. Run a cord from the top corner of one post to the top corner of the other. Repeat for the other side and for the lower crossbars. For easy access to plants, remove the cords when it's time to prune.

Blueberry Basics

Blueberry plants don't bear fruit until they're 3 or 4 years old, so you might want to skip them if patience isn't one of your virtues. But if you're willing to wait, you can enjoy your blueberries as ornamentals in the meantime. (Besides the white spring flowers, blueberries often produce outstanding fall color.)

Highbush blueberries (*Vaccinium corymbosum*)—the most popular home-garden blueberries—can grow in Northern gardens as cold as Zone 3 or as warm as Zone 8. Lowbush blueberries (*V. angustifolium*) will produce small but flavorful fruit in Zones 2 to 6. Rabbiteye blueberries (*V. ashei*) are better adapted to the heat of Zones 7 to 9, as long as they get some frost during winter.

All species need a moist but loose-textured soil high in organic matter, with a pH of 4.5 to 5.2. If a soil test shows that your soil has a pH of 6.2 or higher, it's probably not worth the trouble of adjusting the soil pH. If the pH is less than 6.2, mixing some sphagnum peat moss into the soil at planting time may do the trick.

Most blueberries are not self-fertile, so you'll need to plant at least two, and preferably three, cultivars that can cross-pollinate for good fruit set.

Strawberries Made Simple

There's nothing like the taste of a fresh-picked, sun-warmed, juicy, ripe strawberry. Fortunately, you can

Raspberries need full sun and well-drained soil. For the best fruit, start with virus-free nursery plants and add a generous layer of organic mulch like straw after planting.

Blueberries are great for a low-maintenance landscape. Besides providing fruit, they are attractive as ornamentals.

enjoy this pleasure for yourself without a lot of work.

June-bearing strawberries produce one big crop in early summer. Ever-bearing strawberries produce smaller spring and fall crops. Both types spread by runners, which grow from the mother plant and set down roots.

A relatively low-maintenance and space-saving planting method is the matted row system. Start with the plants in rows 4 feet (1.2 m) apart. Within the rows, space June-bearing cultivars every 18 inches (45 cm) and ever-bearing cultivars every 12 inches (30 cm). For easier harvesting, limit the bed to three rows, leaving enough room at the front, back, and sides for runners.

Pinch the flowers off June-bearing plants the first year, so they put energy into their roots. For ever-bearing, pinch off flowers only until the first of July. Throughout the season, let the runners fill in with new plants wherever they take root. In the fall, keep the plants watered to increase the next year's crop. Mulch with 2 to 3 inches (5 to 7.5 cm) of clean straw to prevent winter damage.

The second summer after planting, rejuvenate the bed right after harvest by setting your lawn mower at 2½ inches (6 cm) and mowing over the whole bed. Rake up the debris, then narrow the width of each row to 12 inches (30 cm) by tilling or turning under the plants on the edges. Spread compost over the bed, and water the plants well to encourage new growth. Depending on how healthy and productive your cultivar is, you can get 3 years or more of harvest. To ensure an ongoing supply, start a new bed in a different spot every 2 to 3 years. When you are finished with the first bed, dig it under and plant it with another crop until the new bed is exhausted.

Rabbiteye blueberries are ideal for warm, Southern gardens.

Highbush blueberries can adapt to a wide range of climates.

Hardy lowbush blueberries grow best in cool-climate areas.

Asparagus officinalis   Liliaceae

ASPARAGUS

There's nothing quite like the taste of fresh-picked asparagus to liven up a spring meal. Plant this perennial once and you'll be able to harvest it for years.

BEST CLIMATE AND SITE: Zones 3–7. Full sun; well-drained soil that's high in organic matter. In the southern part of this range, look for cultivars that tolerate mild winters, such as 'UC 157'.

EDIBLE PARTS: The young shoots, called spears.

GROWING GUIDELINES: Enrich planting bed with rotted manure or compost. Buy and plant year-old crowns about 6–8 inches (15–20 cm) deep and 15 inches (38 cm) apart. Mulch thickly to discourage weeds. Fertilize in spring and fall with rotted manure or fish emulsion. Water during drought for several years after planting.

HARVESTING: Harvest lightly for 2–3 weeks the second year after planting in warm climates; wait an additional year to harvest in cool climates. Once the plants are growing strongly, your harvest season will be about 6 weeks a year. Pick the tender, plump spears that arise in spring by twisting them off at the base when they are 6–8 inches (15–20 cm) high. Leave the skinny, fibrous ones.

PEST AND DISEASE PREVENTION: Buy rust-resistant cultivars. If the soil is poorly drained, plant in raised beds. To eliminate overwintering sites of asparagus beetles, destroy the yellow foliage in fall. Spray serious beetle infestations with rotenone during the growing season.

OTHER COMMENTS: 'Martha Washington' and 'Mary Washington' are rust-resistant.

Ocimum basilicum   Labiatae

BASIL

Basil is a popular annual herb that adds a distinctive taste to tomato-based dishes. Pinch off the flower buds as they form to encourage the production of more leaves.

BEST CLIMATE AND SITE: This annual will grow in all Zones but prefers the warmth of Zones 4–10. Grow during the frost-free growing season. Full sun; well-drained, rich soil.

EDIBLE PARTS: Fragrant and flavorful foliage.

GROWING GUIDELINES: It's easiest to grow basil from a small nursery seedling, but you also can start it from seed. Space plants 6 inches (15 cm) apart. Mulch with compost. Water during drought. For a bushier plant, pinch off shoot tips; use the shoots for cooking or salads. Remove spent flower spikes.

HARVESTING: Pick individual leaves or sprigs as you need them. Or to have extra for freezing or drying, cut the plant back by half; it will resprout. Wait 2 days after rainy weather to harvest basil for drying.

PEST AND DISEASE PREVENTION: Plants are generally problem-free.

OTHER COMMENTS: There is a great variety of basil cultivars to choose from: Large-leaved forms such as 'Lettuce-leaved' and 'Mammoth' are great for cooking; mound-forming, little-leaved types such as 'Spicy Globe' and 'Bush Green' are good for using fresh. Purple-leaved forms such as 'Dark Opal' and 'Purple Ruffles' make striking herbal vinegars. Try cultivars with varying flavor like 'Lemon' or 'Licorice'.

Phaseolus spp.   Leguminosae

BEANS

Beans are a staple in many home gardens. To extend your harvest, plant a few bush bean seeds every 2 to 3 weeks; that way, you won't have to pick all the beans at once.

BEST CLIMATE AND SITE: These annuals grow best in Zone 4 and warmer. Grow during the frost-free season. Full sun; warm, well-drained soil.

EDIBLE PARTS: Pods and seeds.

GROWING GUIDELINES: Sow seeds 1 inch (2.5 cm) deep and 3 inches (7.5 cm) apart after the last frost. Plant in double rows to shade out nearby weeds. Provide trellises for climbing pole beans. Plant bush beans every 2–3 weeks until midsummer to extend your harvest season. Water during drought, especially when plants are flowering.

HARVESTING: Bush beans produce most of their crop over a 2–3-week period; pole beans can be productive for 6 weeks. Pick snap beans daily when they are young and tender. Baby beans may be 2 inches (5 cm) long; filet beans may be pencil thick. Some beans, like 'Romano', have a richer flavor if you wait until the seeds grow large but the pod is still succulent. Let shell beans mature fully and dry on the vine.

PEST AND DISEASE PREVENTION: Don't work around beans while their foliage is wet; you could spread diseases. Avoid planting beans or peas in the same bed more than once every 3 years. To control Mexican bean beetles, destroy infested plants and clean up garden debris in fall.

Vaccinium spp.   Ericaceae

BLUEBERRY

Don't forget to include a few blueberry plants in your garden. Besides producing tasty fruit, these trouble-free shrubs have pretty spring flowers and excellent fall color.

BEST CLIMATE AND SITE: Lowbush blueberries (*V. angustifolium*): Zones 2–6; highbush blueberries (*V. corymbosum*): Zones 3–8; rabbiteye blueberries (*V. ashei*): Zones 7–9. All thrive in full sun but also do well in light shade; rich, moist but not water-logged soil with a pH of 4.5–5.

EDIBLE PARTS: Sweet berries.

GROWING GUIDELINES: Choose 2–3-year-old plants of two to three cultivars that can cross-pollinate and grow well in your climate. (Ask your local nursery owner or Cooperative Extension Service to recommend cultivars for your conditions.) Set highbush and rabbiteye plants 5 feet (1.5 m) apart; space lowbush plants 12 inches (30 cm) apart. Mulch and water during drought to pamper their shallow roots. Fertilize with fish emulsion every week for 4 weeks after planting. In following years, fertilize once only during the spring. Prune older plants in early spring. Cut out the oldest branches at their base or at a young side branch. Remove damaged branches anytime.

HARVESTING: Expect to wait several years before the bushes start bearing. Harvest when the berries turn blue, soft, and sweet.

PEST AND DISEASE PREVENTION: Plants are generally problem-free if planted in the right location. If birds develop a taste for your blueberries, protect plants with woven netting.

Rubus spp.   Rosaceae

BRAMBLES

Brambles are easy to grow and yield succulent, flavorful fruit. Ask your local Cooperative Extension Service to recommend cultivars that will thrive in your area.

BEST CLIMATE AND SITE: Red raspberries are hardy into Zone 3; purple and black types are hardy into Zone 4. Plant heat-tolerant cultivars such as 'Comanche', 'Brazos', and 'Bababerry' in Zones 7–8. Blackberries grow well from Zones 5–9. Full sun; well-drained, humus-rich soil.

EDIBLE PARTS: Sweet berries.

GROWING GUIDELINES: Plant raspberries 1–3 feet (30–90 cm) apart; allow 5–6 feet (1.5–1.8 m) between blackberries. Mulch after planting to discourage weeds. Train the canes to a trellis to make harvesting easier. Thin overcrowded and unproductive canes once a year. Remove all canes from fall-bearing cultivars, such as 'Durham' and 'Fall Red', when the leaves drop in fall. Remove canes that have already produced fruit from summer-bearing types such as 'Latham', but leave the young canes to fruit next year. Ever-bearing types such as 'Heritage' and 'Fall Gold' crop twice during the growing season—on year-old wood in summer and on new wood in fall if your frost-free season is long enough. Remove all the canes in late fall if you prefer to harvest one large crop in early fall.

HARVESTING: Pick the berries when they change color and turn soft and sweet.

PEST AND DISEASE PREVENTION: Work among brambles when foliage is dry so you won't spread diseases. Treat aphids with insecticidal soap.

Brassica oleracea, Botrytis group   Cruciferae

BROCCOLI

The crunchy flower buds of broccoli are great in salads and stir fries. Keep cabbageworms and loopers off your crop by protecting plants with floating row covers.

BEST CLIMATE AND SITE: This annual grows best in Zone 3 and warmer. Full sun and cool but not cold weather. Heat-tolerant cultivars can continue producing in warmer weather, especially if in partial shade. Fertile, moist but not wet soil.

EDIBLE PARTS: Vitamin-rich stems and immature flower buds.

GROWING GUIDELINES: Set plants out a month before the average last frost date, spacing them 12–24 inches (30–60 cm) apart. Fertilize with fish emulsion when you plant seedlings and every 3 weeks afterward to keep the plant actively growing. Water if the soil begins to dry out. Mulch to reduce weeds and keep the soil cool.

HARVESTING: Cut off the large central head when it reaches full size and has plump, green flower buds. If you wait until yellow flowers begin to open, you're too late. Leave some stem on the plant and pick the smaller side shoots later.

PEST AND DISEASE PREVENTION: Cover plants with floating row covers to protect them from flea beetles, root maggots, and other pests. Or dust with BT to control cabbageworms and cabbage loopers. Before cooking, soak harvested heads in salt water to chase out caterpillars.

RELATED PLANTS: See the Cabbage entry and the Cauliflower entry on page 142.

Brassica oleracea, Capitata group   Brassicaceae

CABBAGE

For top-quality cabbage, cover plants with row covers to deter pests. Leaving the stem in the ground after harvest may yield a second picking of miniature cabbage heads.

BEST CLIMATE AND SITE: An annual that grows well in Zone 3 and warmer. Full sun in cool weather—the head matures best at about 50°F (10°C). Well-drained, fertile soil for quick-maturing kinds; moister soil for later maturing types.

EDIBLE PARTS: Leafy head

GROWING GUIDELINES: It's easiest to plant nursery seedlings; set them 12–18 inches (30–45 cm) apart. Use fish emulsion as a transplanting solution. Once the plants are growing, side-dress with rotted manure. Mulch to reduce weeds and maintain moist soil. Water when the soil dries out.

HARVESTING: Thin out overcrowded plants and eat the young thinnings. Harvest full-size, firm, round heads before they split. If you leave a green stalk in the garden, it may resprout and produce miniheads.

PEST AND DISEASE PREVENTION: Cover plants with floating row covers to protect them from cabbage maggots, imported cabbageworms, and cabbage loopers. Or use BT for caterpillar pests. To avoid diseases, destroy poorly growing plants and rotate planting sites.

OTHER COMMENTS: Late-maturing cultivars such as 'Custodian' and 'Ruby Perfection' store better than early types. Look for heat-resistant cultivars such as 'Stonehead' if your cool season is short.

RELATED PLANTS: See the Broccoli entry and the Cauliflower entry on page 142.

Daucus carota var. *sativus*　　　Umbelliferae

CARROT

The key to great carrots is deep, loose soil. If your soil is shallow, try building raised beds to provide extra rooting room or plant short-rooted cultivars.

BEST CLIMATE AND SITE: This annual performs best in Zone 3 and warmer. Grow during the cool growing season. Full sun; light, deep, loose soil of average fertility. If your soil is heavy or thin, raise the planting bed and amend the soil with well-decayed compost (not manure, which can lead to deformed roots).

EDIBLE PARTS: Sweet, vitamin-rich root.

GROWING GUIDELINES: Sow seed ½ inch (1 cm) deep in early spring and cover the bed with a floating row cover to help keep the soil loose, so the seedlings emerge easily. Thin overcrowded seedlings so remaining plants stand 2–3 inches (5–7.5 cm) apart. Mulch lightly to keep the soil cool and moist.

HARVESTING: For best flavor, let roots mature to their full size, but pick them while still tender. Pull and sample a few to see if they are ready.

PEST AND DISEASE PREVENTION: With the right soil and floating row covers, generally problem-free.

OTHER COMMENTS: Use short-rooted cultivars like 'Orbit' or 'Planet' in shallow soils.

Brassica oleracea, Botrytis group　　　Cruciferae

CAULIFLOWER

Although white is the most common color for cauliflower, you may want to grow green or purple cultivars that don't need blanching. Or try self-blanching white cultivars.

BEST CLIMATE AND SITE: This annual grows best in Zone 3 and warmer. Plant seedlings while the weather is cool (50°–60°F/10°–15°C) but frost-free. Full sun or light shade in warmer weather; rich, moist soil.

EDIBLE PARTS: Dense white heads (actually immature flower buds).

GROWING GUIDELINES: Set plants out around the average date for the last spring frost in your area. Space them 18–36 inches (45–90 cm) apart. Water during dry weather. Feed once a month with fish emulsion, or use seaweed extract if leaf tips or heads begin to brown. Blanch white-headed cultivars to prevent from turning green in the sun. Here's how: On a dry, sunny day, pull the outer leaves over a newly swelling head to keep sunlight out. Tie the leaf tips together with a rubber band or twist tie. You can skip this step if you grow self-blanching, green- or purple-headed cultivars.

HARVESTING: Cut off the head when it is full but before the buds begin to separate and thin out.

PEST AND DISEASE PREVENTION: Cover plants with floating row covers to avoid flea beetles, cabbage maggots, and caterpillars.

OTHER COMMENTS: Ask local gardeners or your Cooperative Extension Service which cultivars grow well in your area. If you have a short cool season, you'll want a quick-cropping cultivar.

Prunus spp.   Rosaceae

CHERRY, BUSH

Bush cherries produce sweet, juicy fruit on low, spreading plants, making the harvest much easier than with tree cherries. The plants also offer white flowers in spring.

BEST CLIMATE AND SITE: Sand cherry (*Prunus besseyi*): Zones 3–6; Nanking cherry (*P. tomentosa*): Zones 3–8. Full sun; fertile, well-drained soil for the best yield. Both flower early in the growing season; set in an area protected from late-spring frosts. Both tolerate heat; Nanking cherry also tolerates drought.

EDIBLE PARTS: Sweet cherries.

GROWING GUIDELINES: Thin out old or overcrowded branches in early spring. Plant two compatible cultivars for cross-pollination or buy a self-compatible cultivar.

HARVESTING: Pick fruits when they become soft and sweet. Sand cherries will turn purple-black; Nanking cherries will turn bright red.

PEST AND DISEASE PREVENTION: Bush cherries are less susceptible to plum curculio, peachtree borer, and brown rot than cherry trees, but you still may see any of these problems. To avoid plum curculio, destroy fallen fruit, which could have larvae inside or carry brown rot spores. Avoid brown rot by providing free air circulation and spraying after flowering with sulfur, a protective fungicide. To avoid peachtree borers, keep the bushes growing vigorously. Don't damage the trunk with a lawn mower or string timmer. If borers do tunnel into the wood, spear them by sticking a stiff wire into the borer hole.

Allium schoenoprasum   Liliaceae

CHIVES

Chives form perennial clumps of onion-flavored leaves and flowers. Add the leaves during the last few minutes of cooking; toss the flowers into salads or use as a garnish.

BEST CLIMATE AND SITE: Zones 3–9. Full sun; tolerates light shade. Grows best in well-drained, rich soil of average fertility; tolerates light or heavy soil.

EDIBLE PARTS: Onion-flavored leaves and flowers.

GROWING GUIDELINES: Plant seedlings, seed, or divisions—all grow easily. Space plants 5–8 inches (12–20 cm) apart. Remove the lavender-colored flowers before they go to seed to prevent the spread of volunteer chive seedlings. Divide to reinvigorate older clumps. Pot up a division or volunteer seedling and move it to a sunny windowsill for winter harvests.

HARVESTING: Cut off individual leaves as needed or cut the entire plant down 3 inches (7.5 cm) from the ground—it will resprout.

PEST AND DISEASE PREVENTION: Plants are generally problem-free.

RELATED PLANTS:
GARLIC CHIVES (*A. tuberosum*): White flowers and flat, garlic-flavored leaves.
See also the Garlic entry on page 146 and the Onion entry on page 147.

Zea mays   Gramineae

CORN

Growing sweet corn may take some extra care, but most gardeners agree that it's worth the effort. Plant early-season, midseason, and late-maturing types to have corn all summer.

BEST CLIMATE AND SITE: Annual that grows best in Zone 3 and warmer. Plant during the frost-free growing season. Full sun; rich, moist soil. Protect from high winds.

EDIBLE PARTS: Sweet succulent seeds.

GROWING GUIDELINES: Sow seed 1 inch (2.5 cm) deep and 4 inches (10 cm) apart after the average date of the last spring frost in your area. To ensure good wind pollination, plant seed in at least four rows of four plants each. Or plant in clusters of four, spaced 1½ feet (45 cm) apart, with several feet (1–2 m) in between each cluster. Mulch once the seedlings emerge to suppress weeds. Mound soil up around the base of the stalks for more stability. Fertilize with rotted manure or fish emulsion every 3 weeks. Water during dry weather.

HARVESTING: Corn will ripen several weeks after the silks appear. Puncture one kernal: If it's full of milky sap, it's ready. Eat promptly.

PEST AND DISEASE PREVENTION: To discourage corn earworms, put mineral oil on the corn silks after they wilt. Spray BT into borer holes in corn stalks. To keep raccoons from peeling off ears, use strong packaging tape to hold the top of the ear closed and secure the bottom of the ear to the stalk.

OTHER COMMENTS: If you sometimes refrigerate corn, grow extended sugar cultivars such as 'Sugar Buns' and 'Duet' that stay sweeter longer.

Cucumis sativus   Curcurbitaceae

CUCUMBER

It's quicker to start with nursery-grown cucumber seedlings in peat pots, though plants will also grow easily from seed. Let vines creep or train them up a trellis.

BEST CLIMATE AND SITE: Annual that grows best in Zone 4 and warmer. Full sun; fertile, moist soil.

EDIBLE PARTS: Juicy fruit.

GROWING GUIDELINES: Enrich the planting bed with plenty of organic matter. Plant once the danger of spring frost passes and the soil is warm. Sow seed ½ inch (1 cm) deep, with 3–5 seeds per foot of row. Thin seedlings or set out plants to stand 1 foot (30 cm) apart. Mulch after planting and water whenever the soil begins to dry out. Fertilize with fish emulsion every 2 weeks.

HARVESTING: Harvest every 1–2 days. Cut fruits off the vine while the flesh is firm. Harvest pickling types when they are several inches (15–20 cm) long. Let slicing types round out at the unattached end before picking.

PEST AND DISEASE PREVENTION: To avoid diseases, plant disease-resistant cultivars such as 'Jazzer', 'Sweet Success Hybrid', and 'Saladin Hybrid', and rotate crops. Don't work among the vines when they are wet. Use floating row covers over young plants to keep out cucumber beetles and the bacterial wilt they carry. Uncover plants when they start to flower so they can be pollinated by insects. Spray beetles with pyrethrin.

OTHER COMMENTS: In small gardens, look for compact bush cultivars such as 'Bush Pickle', 'Salad Bush Hybrid', and 'Bush Champion'.

| _Ribes_ spp. | Grossulariaceae | _Anethum graveolens_ | Umbelliferae |

CURRANTS

The tart berries of currants are excellent for jam or juice. Plant two or more cultivars if possible; cross-pollination will increase yields. Prune for good air circulation.

BEST CLIMATE AND SITE: Zones 3–5 are best; plants struggle in heat. Full sun or light shade; moist, even heavy, but not swampy soil. The bushes can grow up to 5 feet (1.5 m) high with an equal spread.

EDIBLE PARTS: The berries, which ripen to white, black, red, pink, green, or gold.

GROWING GUIDELINES: Early fall planting is best. Set black currant plants 3–4 inches (7.5–10 cm) deeper than they were growing at the nursery; plant others 1 inch (2.5 cm) lower. Space plants 5–7 feet (1.5–2.1) apart. Mulch after planting to discourage weeds. Water during drought. Fertilize monthly with fish emulsion. Thin out old or poorly producing branches to allow vigorous new wood to grow.

HARVESTING: Let the berries ripen completely for the best flavor. Pick the entire cluster, then separate berries.

PEST AND DISEASE PREVENTION: Use rust-resistant cultivars such as 'Crusader' or 'Consort' if white pine blister rust is a problem in your area. Currants may be banned from your state if there is potential for severe pine damage from this disease. Thin overgrown shrubs to encourage air circulation and discourage mildew.

RELATED PLANTS: See the Gooseberries entry on page 146.

DILL

Dill is a fast-growing annual herb that produces flavorful leaves and seeds. The tiny yellow flowers will attract many kinds of beneficial insects to your garden.

BEST CLIMATE AND SITE: This annual can grow in all Zones, but Zones 2–9 are best. Full sun; well-drained soil of average fertility.

EDIBLE PARTS: Flavorful ferny leaves, flowers, and seeds.

GROWING GUIDELINES: Sow seed ¼ inch (6 mm) deep and 4–8 inches (5–10 cm) apart, starting in early spring. Plant a few seeds every 2 weeks during the frost-free growing season for fresh dill all summer. Mulch to reduce weeds.

HARVESTING: Pick off individual leaves and flowers. Or cut the entire plant back by half and let it resprout. For dill seeds, let the flowers mature until they contain firm brown seeds. But pick the seed clusters before the seeds spill out. Let them finish drying in a paper bag.

PEST AND DISEASE PREVENTION: Plants are generally problem-free.

OTHER COMMENTS: If you have trouble with dill growing too tall and falling over, plant newer compact cultivars such as 'Bouquet' and 'Fernleaf'.

| *Allium sativum* | Liliaceae | *Ribes hirtellum* | Grossulariaceae |

GARLIC

GOOSEBERRIES

Grow garlic for its tangy greens and pungent bulbs. For best results, plant cloves in fall and mulch them over winter. When the leaves turn brown, it's time to harvest.

BEST CLIMATE AND SITE: Zones 5–10. Full sun; light, fertile soil.

EDIBLE PARTS: Bulbs and pungent greens.

GROWING GUIDELINES: Look for cultivars that are suited to your growing conditions. For the West Coast, try 'Silverskin' or 'California Early'. In the eastern states, try 'Valencia'. Plant bulbs 2 inches (5 cm) deep and 6 inches (15 cm) apart in fall and cover the bed with mulch. In spring, apply fish emulsion fertilizer every 2 weeks and water if the soil begins to get dry. Pull or cut off weeds that emerge through the mulch.

HARVESTING: Dig the bulbs in late summer or fall when the leaves turn brown. Cure in a hot, dry location for several weeks before storing. Snip a leaf or two from plants as needed; use like chives, or chop greens up with olive oil and grated cheese for a tangy garlic pesto.

PEST AND DISEASE PREVENTION: To avoid diseases, plant in well-drained soil. If problems occur, rotate the planting site.

RELATED PLANTS: See the Onion entry.

If you want to enjoy the sweet taste of gooseberries, you'll have to grow them yourself—the soft fruits don't pack or ship well. Wear gloves when picking to avoid the spines.

BEST CLIMATE AND SITE: Zones 3–6 are best; plants struggle in heat. Full sun or light shade; fertile, well-drained soil.

EDIBLE PARTS: Berries.

GROWING GUIDELINES: Plant and grow gooseberries much like currants (see page 145). To prevent leaf-edge browning, add dolomitic limestone or Epsom salts to the soil. Trim side branches back in mid-summer. Remove unproductive canes in fall.

HARVESTING: Pick the berries when they become soft and sweet. Wear gloves when harvesting to avoid the spines.

PEST AND DISEASE PREVENTION: See the Currants entry on page 145.

OTHER COMMENTS: Can self-pollinate, so you can plant as few as one bush. But for an extended harvest, grow early-season, midseason, and late-producing cultivars.

RELATED PLANTS:

EUROPEAN GOOSEBERRY (*R. uva-crispa*): Produces larger berries but can be troubled by mildew.

| *Lactuca sativa* | Compositae | *Allium cepa* | Liliaceae |

LETTUCE

Crisp lettuce grows best when temperatures are cool. In warm climates, a fall sowing can give you an early spring harvest; elsewhere, plant in early spring and midsummer.

BEST CLIMATE AND SITE: You can raise this annual in all Zones. Grows best in cool temperatures and full sun; light shade in hot temperatures. Fertile, moist, but not wet soil.

EDIBLE PARTS: Leaves or leafy head.

GROWING GUIDELINES: Scatter seeds thinly over the planting bed and rake lightly to cover them. Starting in early spring, plant seeds or seedlings every 2 weeks during cool, mild weather. Thin plants to stand 8–10 inches (20–25 cm) apart. Fertilize with fish emulsion every 2 weeks if needed to keep the plants growing quickly, or mulch with compost. Water if the soil begins to dry out.

HARVESTING: Pick individual leaves or harvest an entire plant. Cut off the rosettes of leafy types or the heads of heading types when they get full but before they send up a flowering stalk and become bitter.

PEST AND DISEASE PREVENTION: To avoid rot or mold diseases, plant in well-drained soil, thin overcrowded plants, and rotate planting sites.

OTHER COMMENTS: If you have a short cool season, grow cultivars such as 'Red Sails', 'Lollo Rossa', and 'Summertime' that tolerate heat. Red or frilly-leaved types can double as ornamentals.

ONION

Dried or fresh, raw or cooked, onions are an indispensable ingredient in many foods. Pick the young greens for scallions, or wait for the tops to turn brown to harvest the bulbs.

BEST CLIMATE AND SITE: Grow onions in all Zones for scallions; Zone 3 and warmer for bulbs. Full sun; fertile, light soil rich in organic matter.

EDIBLE PARTS: Pungent bulb; tangy greens.

GROWING GUIDELINES: Choose a cultivar that is appropriate for your climate. In the North, plant long-day onions in spring. In the South, grow short-day onions during fall and winter. It's easiest to start with small bulbs called "sets," but you will be limited to fewer types. Alternatively, buy nursery seedlings. Space sets or transplants 2 inches (5 cm) deep and 4–6 inches (10–14 cm) apart. After planting, mulch with compost. Pull or cut off any weeds that emerge through the mulch. Water if the soil begins to dry out.

HARVESTING: Harvest young green onions for scallions. Or harvest the bulbs when the tops brown and flop. Cure them in a warm, dry location for several weeks.

PEST AND DISEASE PREVENTION: If onion fly is a problem in your area, keep the crop covered with floating row covers. Rotate the planting site regularly.

RELATED PLANTS: See the Garlic entry and the Chives entry on page 143.

Petroselinum crispum　　　Umbelliferae

PARSLEY

Parsley produces a lush crop of flavorful, vitamin-packed leaves its first year. Plants may live over winter and will produce flowers and seeds the following year.

BEST CLIMATE AND SITE: Zones 5–9. Full sun or light shade; deep, fertile soil.

EDIBLE PARTS: Vitamin-packed leaves.

GROWING GUIDELINES: Parsley is easiest to start from nursery seedlings. Space plants 8 inches (20 cm) apart. Plants may self-sow the second year. Fertilize in late spring and summer with fish emulsion. Pull any nearby weeds. Set out new plants each year.

HARVESTING: Pick larger outer leaves one by one or cut the entire plant back. It may resprout.

PEST AND DISEASE PREVENTION: Plants are generally problem-free.

OTHER COMMENTS: Choose from curly-leaved decorative types, flat-leaved, full-flavored Italian parsley, or carrot-rooted Hamburg parsley.

Pisum sativum　　　Leguminosae

PEA

Peas are a classic crop for the spring garden. Look for edible-podded types—like snow peas and stringless cultivars of snap peas—to save time in the kitchen.

BEST CLIMATE AND SITE: This annual grows best in Zone 2 and warmer. Grow during cool but not cold weather. Full sun; light, well-drained soil. You can plant in heavier soil if you start a late-season crop in the warmth of summer. Shelter from strong winds.

EDIBLE PARTS: Seeds and, in some cases, the young pods.

GROWING GUIDELINES: Sow seed 1 inch (2.5 cm) deep and 1 inch (2.5 cm) apart in early spring. Plant early-season, midseason, and late-maturing cultivars for an extended harvest of fresh peas. Try heat-tolerant strains if you have a short cool season. Install a trellis for taller-growing peas. Lower-yielding dwarf types may support themselves if you plant a double row. After the seedlings are up, mulch around them to keep down weeds. Water during drought.

HARVESTING: Pick shelling peas daily once the seeds are swollen but before the pod loses its gloss. Pick snow peas while the seeds are still small and the pod is flat. Let snap peas grow until the pods are rounded but still smooth to enjoy sweet peas and the succulent pod.

PEST AND DISEASE PREVENTION: Spray insecticidal soap on thrips or aphids. To prevent diseases, plant in well-drained soil and rotate the planting site.

Capsicum annuum var. _annuum_　　　Solanaceae

PEPPER

Garden peppers come in a variety of shapes, colors, and flavors. Pick sweet or bell peppers when they are green, or leave them on the plant to develop their color.

BEST CLIMATE AND SITE: Although peppers are actually perennial, they are best grown as annuals in Zone 4 and warmer. Grow in warm, frost-free weather; full sun and fertile, well-drained soil.

EDIBLE PARTS: Sweet or spicy fruit.

GROWING GUIDELINES: Set plants out 10–15 inches (25–30 cm) apart when the danger of frost is well past and the soil is warm. Mulch seedlings with compost after planting. If growth slows, fertilize with a diluted solution of fish emulsion. Water during dry weather.

HARVESTING: Cut peppers off while green for a tangy flavor or let them ripen completely for a sweet flavor. Hot peppers reach full spiciness if you let them ripen completely in hot, sunny weather.

PEST AND DISEASE PREVENTION: Plant in well-drained soil to avoid root rot. Rotate plantings.

OTHER COMMENTS: Pick from peppers with ultrahot, sweet, and intermediate flavors. For colorful peppers, let fruits ripen completely. Try orange 'Gypsy Hybrid', red 'Sweet Banana', yellow 'Lemon Belle Hybrid', purple 'Lilac Belle Hybrid', or brown 'Sweet Chocolate'.

RELATED PLANTS: See the Tomato entry on page 153 and the Potato entry.

Solanum tuberosum　　　Solanaceae

POTATO

Potatoes produce their best crops where the soil is light and loose. If your soil is heavy or shallow, plant raised beds and add ample amounts of compost.

BEST CLIMATE AND SITE: Plant this annual in Zone 3 and warmer. Grow during warm weather. Full sun; deep, light, fertile soil.

EDIBLE PARTS: Starchy underground tuber.

GROWING GUIDELINES: If your soil is heavy or shallow, plant in raised beds and add plenty of compost. Grow potatoes from pieces of tuber called "seed potatoes." Cut seed potatoes so each piece has at least one "eye," and let them cure in a warm place before planting; or plant whole seed potatoes, which don't need curing. Set them about 5 inches (12.5 cm) deep and 1 foot (30 cm) apart. Mound soil or decaying straw over the base of the vines as they grow upward. This keeps soil moist and cool; tubers may even grow in the mound.

HARVESTING: Unearth tender new potatoes about the time the vines flower. Or dig fully mature potatoes once the vines die back. Cure the tubers for 3 weeks in total darkness, 55°F (13°C), and high humidity. Store in a cool, dark area.

PEST AND DISEASE PREVENTION: To prevent diseases, plant only certified, disease-free tubers. Use disease-resistant cultivars if you've had an earlier disease problem. Rotate new plantings. Destroy any rotten tubers or vines. Use pyrethrin powder on Colorado potato beetles.

OTHER COMMENTS: Choose potatoes that have gold, purple, red, or brown skin.

| *Salvia officinalis* | Labiatae | *Rumex* spp. | Polygonaceae |

SAGE

SORREL

Sage is a traditional seasoning for poultry dishes. This shrubby herb is a perennial, but you may need to buy new plants every few years as old ones decline.

BEST CLIMATE AND SITE: Zones 4–8. Full sun; light, well-drained soil.

EDIBLE PARTS: Aromatic leaves.

GROWING GUIDELINES: Start with nursery plants, or sow seed outdoors in early spring ½ inch (1 cm) deep and 3–6 inches (7.5–15 cm) apart. Thin seedlings or space transplants to stand 20–24 inches (50–60 cm) apart. Water during drought. Cut back older stems to side shoots to encourage new growth. Sage is a perennial, but plants often decline after 3–4 years.

HARVESTING: Pick individual leaves or sprigs. Flowering types are most pungent just before they bloom.

PEST AND DISEASE PREVENTION: Plants are generally problem-free.

OTHER COMMENTS: 'Holt's Mammoth' sage has an extra large leaf and no flowers. Golden, purple, and tricolor sages are more ornamental than flavorful.

Perennial sorrel forms large, leafy clumps in rich, well-drained soil with even moisture. Add a tangy touch to salads and soups with the tender spring leaves.

BEST CLIMATE AND SITE: Zones 5–9. Full sun or light shade; rich, well-drained soil.

EDIBLE PARTS: Lemon-flavored leaves.

GROWING GUIDELINES: Start from nursery plants or direct-sow the seed in spring. Plant seed ¼ inch (6 mm) deep and 2 inches (5 cm) apart. Thin seedlings or space transplants to stand 12–18 inches (30–45 cm) apart. In summer, remove the seed stalks to keep the leaves growing.

HARVESTING: Pick individual leaves. They are most tender in cool weather but still good for cooking in hot weather.

PEST AND DISEASE PREVENTION: Plants are generally problem-free.

Spinacia oleracea   Chenopodiaceae

SPINACH

Spinach needs cool, moist conditions for best growth. In warm temperatures, plant spinach in the shade of taller plants, or protect plants with shade cloth.

BEST CLIMATE AND SITE: This annual will grow in all Zones during the cool growing seasons. Full sun; rich, moist, fertile soil. In warm weather, light shade can delay bolting (flowering and seed setting, which signal the end of your harvest).

EDIBLE PARTS: Succulent leaves.

GROWING GUIDELINES: Plant seed ½ inch (1 cm) deep and 2 inches (5 cm) apart every 2 weeks in spring or fall—winter in the South. Once the seedlings are up and growing, mulch with compost, thin to stand 4–6 inches (10–15 cm) apart, and fertilize with fish emulsion. Water if the soil begins to dry out.

HARVESTING: Pick individual outer leaves. Or cut off the entire plant when it forms a full rosette but before it sends up a flowering stalk.

PEST AND DISEASE PREVENTION: Buy disease-resistant cultivars. Thin plants for good air circulation. Keep pests off plants with floating row covers.

OTHER COMMENTS: Smooth-leaved cultivars, like 'Space' and 'Nordic', are easier to wash. Plant slow-bolting cultivars, such as 'Tyee' and 'Indian Summer' if your cool season is short.

Cucurbita spp.   Cucurbitaceae

SQUASH

Squash is an easy, productive crop, but it can take up a lot of valuable room. If space is limited, try compact bush cultivars. Keep plants well mulched for best yields.

BEST CLIMATE AND SITE: This annual grows best in Zone 3 and warmer. Grow in warm, frost-free weather. Full sun; fertile, rich, moist soil.

EDIBLE PARTS: Mild to sweet fruit and large flowers.

GROWING GUIDELINES: Add plenty of compost to the planting site. It's quicker to plant nursery seedlings although seed starts fairly easily. Plant seeds directly a week after the average date for the last frost in your area. Sow them ½ inch (1 cm) deep. Space vining cultivars 3–4 feet (90–120 cm) apart; space bush types 2–3 feet (60–90 cm) apart. Once the plants are growing strongly, fertilize with fish emulsion and mulch. Water if the soil begins to dry out. You can train long vines onto a trellis. Or save time by growing compact cultivars.

HARVESTING: Cut summer squash off the vine when the fruit is young and tender. Let winter squash mature to a hard shell. Cut it with a stem 2–3 inches (5–7.5 cm) long.

PEST AND DISEASE PREVENTION: To discourage diseases, water at ground level, don't walk among the plants when the leaves are wet, and plant disease-resistant cultivars such as 'Sweet Mama'. Rotate new plantings. Protect young plants from pests with floating row covers; remove the covers when plants start to flower.

Fragaria vesca   Rosaceae

STRAWBERRY, ALPINE

The fruits of alpine strawberries may be small, but they offer a big taste. The compact, runnerless plants make a tidy edging for vegetable, herb, and flower gardens.

BEST CLIMATE AND SITE: Zones 4–8. Full sun; average, well-drained soil.

EDIBLE PARTS: Sweet berries.

GROWING GUIDELINES: Set out nursery-grown plants 6–8 inches (15–20 cm) apart in spring. Mulch around them with compost. Water during drought.

HARVESTING: You can pick the fruit all summer long. For best flavor, wait until it has changed color and softened.

PEST AND DISEASE PREVENTION: Plants are generally problem-free.

OTHER COMMENTS: If you have trouble with birds eating red-fruited types, look for varieties with yellow berries such as 'Pineapple Crush'.

RELATED PLANTS:

GARDEN STRAWBERRIES: Bear larger berries in June or through the summer. See "Strawberries Made Simple" on page 136 for growing information.

Helianthus annuus   Compositae

SUNFLOWER

Sunflowers serve a double purpose in the garden: You can admire their bright yellow flowers in summer and harvest the seeds in fall for eating or for bird food.

BEST CLIMATE AND SITE: Grow this annual in Zone 5 and warmer during the warm part of the growing season. Full sun; well-drained soil of average fertility. Protect from strong winds.

EDIBLE PARTS: Protein-rich seeds.

GROWING GUIDELINES: Sow seed in warm soil, after all danger of frost. Plant seed ½ inch (1 cm) deep and 6 inches (15 cm) apart. Thin to stand 18–24 inches (45–60 cm) apart. Water during drought.

HARVESTING: Cut off the flower heads with about 1 foot (30 cm) of stalk as soon as the seed coats harden. Hang the heads or lay them on newspaper to dry in a well-ventilated area.

PEST AND DISEASE PREVENTION: Tie a cloth bag over maturing heads to keep birds away from the seeds.

Thymus spp.   Labiatae   *Lycopersicon esculentum*   Solanaceae

THYME

Thyme is a problem-free perennial that needs full sun and well-drained soil. Grow it in your herb or vegetable garden, or try it as a groundcover on a hot, sunny slope.

BEST CLIMATE AND SITE: Zones 5–9. Full sun; light, well-drained soil. Perennial.

EDIBLE PARTS: Aromatic leaves.

GROWING GUIDELINES: Set out nursery-grown plants 1 foot (30 cm) apart. Many forms will spread aggressively. Allow room to roam unless you want to cut them back often. Remove the old flowers when they are spent. Divide the clump to renew it every 5 years.

HARVESTING: Trim off sprigs as needed. The flavor is most intense before the flower buds open.

PEST AND DISEASE PREVENTION: Plants are generally problem-free.

OTHER COMMENTS: For beautiful foliage and some variety in flavor, look for variegated lemon or silver thyme.

RELATED PLANTS: See the Mother-of-Thyme (*Thymus serpyllum*) entry on page 56.

TOMATO

What would summer be without the taste of fresh-picked, vine-ripened tomatoes? Give plants full sun, even moisture, and a generous layer of mulch for best growth.

BEST CLIMATE AND SITE: Though tomatoes are perennial in hot climates, they are usually grown as annuals in Zone 3 and warmer. Grow during the warm, frost-free growing season. Sun; fertile, well-drained soil.

EDIBLE PARTS: Juicy fruits.

GROWING GUIDELINES: Plant nursery seedlings 18–24 inches (45–60 cm) apart, sinking barren bottom portions of the stem into the soil. Cage tall cultivars. Fertilize with fish emulsion after planting and mulch with compost. Reapply fish emulsion when the first fruits appear. Water during dry weather.

HARVESTING: Twist or snip off ripe fruits when they soften and turn red, pink, orange, or yellow.

PEST AND DISEASE PREVENTION: Use disease-resistant cultivars such as 'Viva Italia Hybrid', 'Lady Luck Hybrid', and 'Celebrity Hybrid'. Rotate the planting site. Brown or black patches at the bottom of the fruit indicate blossom end rot, a cultural problem due to uneven soil moisture and calcium deficiency. Pick off damaged fruit and try to keep the soil evenly moist.

OTHER COMMENTS: Determinate tomatoes stay more compact but produce all their fruit at once. Indeterminate tomatoes, which continue to grow and produce new tomatoes, grow lankier and produce fruit longer.

USDA
PLANT HARDINESS ZONE MAP

The map that follows shows the United States and Canada divided into 10 zones. Each zone is based on a 10°F (5.6°C) difference in average annual minimum temperature. Some areas are considered too high in elevation for plant cultivation and so are not assigned to any zone. There are also island zones that are warmer or cooler than surrounding areas because of differences in elevation; they have been given a zone different from the surrounding areas. Many large urban areas are in a warmer zone than the surrounding land.

Plants grow best within an optimum range of temperatures. The range may be wide for some species and narrow for others. Plants also differ in their ability to survive frost and in their sun or shade requirements.

The zone ratings indicate conditions where designated plants will grow well and not merely survive. Refer to the map to find out which zone you are in. In the low-maintenance plant by plant guides, you'll find recommendations for the plants that grow best in your zone.

Many plants may survive in zones warmer or colder than their recommended zone range. Remember that other factors, including wind, soil type, soil moisture and drainage capability, humidity, snow, and winter sunshine, may have a great effect on growth.

Average annual minimum temperature (°F/°C)

Zone 1	Below -50°F/-45°C	Zone 6	0° to -10°F/-18° to -23°C
Zone 2	-40° to -50°F/-40° to -45°C	Zone 7	10° to 0°F/-12° to -18°C
Zone 3	-30° to -40°F/-34° to -40°C	Zone 8	20° to 10°F/-7° to -12°C
Zone 4	-20° to -30°F/-29° to -34°C	Zone 9	30° to 20°F/-1° to -7°C
Zone 5	-10° to -20°F/-23° to -29°C	Zone 10	40° to 30°F/4° to -1°C

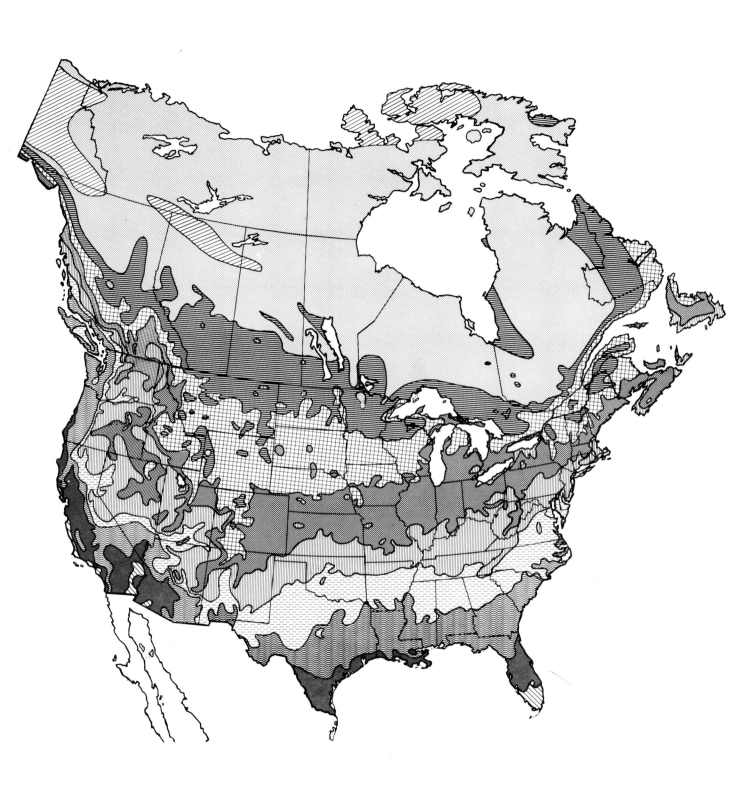

INDEX

The numbers in bold indicate main entries, and the numbers in italic indicate illustrations.

ACKNOWLEDGMENTS

Photo Credits

Ardea: photographer Kenneth W. Fink: copyright page; photographer François Gohier: page 8; photographer Allen Paterson: page 94 (top); and photographer John Mason: page 152 (left).

Auscape: photographer Jerry Harpur: front cover and page 12.

Gillian Beckett: page 55 (right).

Bruce Coleman: photographer Hans Reinhard: half title page and page 92 (bottom); photographer Eric Crichton: title page and page 15 (top); and photographer Jules Cowan: page 58.

John Callanan: pages 34 (left), 37 (left), 60 (top), 82 (right), and 86 (left).

Michael Dirr: page 72 (left).

Thomas Eltzroth: back cover (top), contents page (right), pages 14, 18 (top), 20 (right), 26, 31 (left and right), 32 (left), 35 (left), 36 (left), 38 (left), 43, 51 (left), 52 (left and right), 53 (left), 54 (left), 55 (left), 62, 72 (right), 77 (right), 82 (left), 90, 94 (bottom), 96, 98 (bottom), 102 (left and right), 103 (right), 104 (left), 106 (left), 107 (right), 108 (left), 111 (left), 113 (left), 114 (right), 116 (left and right), 117 (right), 120 (left), 121 (right), 122 (left and right), 123 (right), 127 (bottom), 136, 137, 138, 140 (left), 143 (right), 144 (right), 146 (right), 148 (left), 151 (left), and 153 (right).

Derek Fell: pages 30 (right), 38 (right), 39 (left), 53 (right), 54 (right), 60 (bottom), 69 (right), 80 (left), 88 (right), 143 (left), and 146 (left).

The Garden Picture Library: contents page (top) and page 24 (right); photographer Clive Nichols: back cover (bottom) and page 135; photographer John Glover: opposite title page, pages 22, 80 (right), 93, 128, and 129 (left); photographer Lamontagne: pages 15 (bottom), 29 (right), 64 (bottom), and 147 (right); photographer J. Legate: page 17 (left); photographer Steven Wooster: pages 21 (bottom), 97, and 99; photographer Henk Dijkman: page 24 (left); photographer J. S. Sira: page 33 (right); photographer John Ainsworth: page 63 (right); photographer Vaughan Fleming: page 95 (bottom); photographer Ron Sutherland: page 111 (right); photographer Neil Holmes: page 124; photographer Bob Challinor: page 123 (left); photographer Brigitte Thomas: pages 127 (top) and 133; and photographers Mayer/Lescanff: page 129 (right).

Jerry Pavia: back cover (center), endpapers, pages 27, 28, 30 (left), 32 (left), 34 (right), 36 (right), 44, 45, 46, 64 (top), 70 (left), 76 (right), 77 (left), 86 (right), 100, 106 (right), 108 (right), 115 (right), 118 (left), 119 (right), 120 (right), and 121 (left).

Joanne Pavia: opposite contents page, pages 40, 47, 49 (left), 61, 71 (right), 73 (right), 79 (right), 83 (left), 85 (left), 89 (left), 104 (right), 110 (right), 112 (left), and 115 (left).

Photos Horticultural: pages 16, 17 (right), 18 (bottom), 19, 20 (left), 21 (top), 35 (right), 39 (right), 42, 66, 67, 69 (left), 78 (right), 87 (left), 92 (top), 95 (top), 98 (top), 103 (left), 119 (left), 131 (left and right), 132, and 134.

Rodale Stock Images: pages 48 and 117 (left).

Harry Smith: pages 11 (left and right), 33 (left), 49 (right), 50 (left and right), 51 (right), 56 (left and right), 57 (left and right), 63 (left), 68, 70 (left and right), 73 (left), 74 (right), 75 (left and right), 76 (left), 78 (left), 79 (left), 81 (left and right), 83 (right), 84 (left and right), 85 (right), 87 (right), 88 (left), 89 (right), 101 (left and right), 105 (left and right), 107 (left), 109 (left and right), 110 (left), 112 (right), 113 (right), 114 (left), 118 (right), 126, 140 (right), and 145 (left).

David Wallace: pages 74 (left), 139 (left and right), 141 (left and right), 142 (left and right), 144 (left), 145 (right), 147 (left), 148 (right), 149 (left and right), 150 (left and right), 151 (right), 152 (right), and 153 (left).

Weldon Russell: contents page (bottom) and page 37 (right).

Ron West: page 29 (left).